Letters from the Antipodes

SOME ENGLISH TRANSLATIONS OF BUTOR'S WORKS

Novels

A Change of Heart (*La Modification*), trans. Jean Stewart. New York: Simon and Schuster, 1958.
Passing Time (*L'Emploi du temps*), trans. Jean Stewart. New York: Simon and Schuster, 1960. London: Calder, 1965.
Degrees (degrés), trans. Richard Howard. New York: Simon and Schuster, 1961. London: Methuen, 1962.

Other Works

Inventory (a selection of Butor's critical writings from *Répertoire* I, II and III by various translators). New York: Simon and Schuster, 1968. London: Cape, 1970.
Mobile, Study for a Representation of the United States (*Mobile, étude pour une représentation des Etats-Unis*), trans. Richard Howard. New York: Simon and Schuster, 1963.
Niagara (6 810 000 Litres d'eau par seconde), trans. Elinor S. Miller. Chicago: Henry Regnery and Co., 1969.

General Books on Butor in English

Michael Spencer, *Michel Butor*. New York: Twayne Publishers, 1974.
Jennifer Waelti-Walters, *Michel Butor*. Victoria, Canada: Sono Nis Press, 1977.

Michel Butor

Letters from the Antipodes

Translated from Boomerang with an
Introduction and Afterword by
Michael Spencer

Ohio University Press

Athens, Ohio
London

First published in the United States
by Ohio University Press, Athens, Ohio.

ISBN 0 8214 0659 0

© University of Queensland Press, St Lucia, Queensland 1981

Typeset by Savage & Co. Ltd, Brisbane
Printed and bound by Hedges & Bell Pty Ltd, Melbourne

National Library of Australia
Cataloguing-in-Publication data

Butor, Michel, 1926—
    Letters from the Antipodes.

I. Spencer, Michael, 1936—. II. Butor, Michel, 1926—.
Boomerang.   III. Title: Boomerang.   IV. Title.

848'.91407

Contents

Introduction

Australia has never been an object of much curiosity for French writers, partly because its existence was barely known anywhere until the late eighteenth century, partly, one suspects, because the notion of "culture" could be extended to allow explicit or implicit comparisons between France and Persia (Montesquieu), North America (Chateaubriand) or Tahiti (Diderot), whereas the world of the Aborigine fell outside its normal boundaries. In the nineteenth century, two novels by Jules Verne, *Mistress Branican* and *Captain Grant's Children*, partly made amends, although the attitude to Aboriginal culture expressed within them is, to say the least, ambiguous—an ambiguity which "Letters from the Antipodes" fully exploits.[1] A few literary Frenchmen have visited Australia, including the highly eccentric Raymond Roussel, who was impressed gastronomically, but was not moved to write anything—not that this was unusual, since his "travel" books have nothing whatever to do with travel.

Michel Butor lives in Nice, teaches at the University of Geneva, and spends his vacations in central France, writing. Travel, writing and teaching form the substance of his life, along with family interests (he has four daughters), and the relationships between these four facets of a busy and frequently overburdened existence find their way, naturally enough, into his books—although I have no intention of "explaining" the man by the work, or vice versa. In 1968, he visited Australia for the first time and attended Writers' Week at the Adelaide Festival; he returned again in 1971, on a seven week whistle-stop lecture tour taking in New Zealand as well, with a week's vacation in Central Australia; then in 1976, accompanied by his wife, he spent two months as Writer-in-Residence attached to the University of Queensland French Department. It was during this period that a great deal of the research for and some of the writing of "Letters from the Antipodes" was undertaken. He was due to return to the University of Queensland again in 1980, this time as Visiting Professor of Fine Arts, but temporary ill-health obliged him to cancel his trip.

That Butor likes Australia should be obvious from the frequency of his visits. When asked in a recent interview if he wanted to return, and what he hoped to find, he replied: "Yes, I'd like very much to return to Australia. I like Australia very much: it's a country I feel a great affection for. I feel that I'm a pioneer in French literature, that I'm discovering it while at the same time I want to discover much more. If I return what would interest me most would be to get a feeling for Australia's evolution today, especially its cultural evolution ... I would try to discern what new developments there had been in the few years I'd been away—in literature, painting, and so on. Perhaps there won't have been anything of genius, but even if there hasn't been much that's first rate, the way things will have changed will provide me with all sorts of information about what is going on in the world."[2] Much of Butor's work is concerned with this search for new perspectives; having begun his literary career by writing four novels, two of which have already been successfully recuperated as "classics",[3] he abandoned the novelistic medium after 1960 for what are normally known as "mobile" works. In books such as *Mobile* (1962) or *Où* (1971), the page becomes the focal point of a variety of geographical and historical "sites" which engage in a kind of dialogue, creating what might be termed a "relational geography" allowing the reader a plurality of textual itineraries. This point is considered in more detail in the afterword.

Given this highly unusual concept of the (travel) book, it is not surprising that when Butor decided to write about Australia, he should write about other places predominantly in the Southern Hemisphere, setting up a new dialogue and creating a series of perspectives on and from Australia. "Letters from the Antipodes" is part of a far longer work in seven interwoven sections entitled *Boomerang*,[4] which concerns itself not only with Australia, but also with parts of South America, Oceania and in particular Tahiti, Singapore and—in the Northern Hemisphere—British Columbia and the United States. The selection is not arbitrary, since the countries are linked thematically, onomastically, and by a series of invented dreams.

One of the themes which has occurred in Butor's writings since his very first novel, *Passage de Milan* (1954), is that of the outcast: Horace Buck, the West Indian living in northern England (*Passing Time*), the North American Indian as an outcast in his own country (*Mobile*) and—in the same work—the Negro; finally, in *Boomerang*, the Australian Aborigine, another stranger in his own land. Other parts of *Boomerang* refer to the Northwest Coast Indian, the American Indian, and the South American Indian, and one of the partial readings of the text could be a comparative one of passages in which their legends and artifacts, and their relationship with White Man, are described. Another theme is travel, and in particular exploration, with the writings of famous navigators re-used, sometimes extensively rewritten, by Butor. Another way of travelling around *Boomerang* is therefore to follow the explorers, whose names are capitalized, forming a network of landmarks or beacons enabling the reader to situate himself. Finally, the dreams form a direct passage from one section of the book to the other, as they consist of episodes already related, but which are re-presented in the form of a dream involving the narrator.

The reader of *Boomerang* can further situate himself by a whole series of other textual signs or markers. He is "in" Australia if the text he is reading is coloured red, and set in one block towards the top of the page with running titles at the bottom; he is "in" the United States if the text is blue, set towards the bottom of the page with running titles at the top, and so on. Within Australia he can still further situate himself by realizing that each time (or nearly each time) he comes to the adjective "red", he is passing from one subject or source-strand to another, while the other sections of *Boomerang* also have "thematic punctuators" in the form of adjectives of colour or recurrent phrases. For one must realize that by far the largest part of "Letters from the Antipodes"—around eighty or ninety per cent—is (mis)quoted material which is juxtaposed, with the rest consisting of narratorial comment, anecdotes and a series of "variations on leitmotifs" such as "on the other side of the world without end", "what are you reading/eating/dreaming about" or "on the wall of my room in college".

"Letters from the Antipodes" draws upon thirty-two different sources, which are listed in full in the afterword. Among the most important are a popularized edition of Captain Cook's Journal, two series of descriptions of bark-paintings, the first erudite, the second less so, a collection of ghost-stories, Australian bank-notes, the foreword to Bougainville's *A Journey round the World*, and the two novels by Jules Verne already mentioned. Other less frequently used sources include massage parlour and dalliance advertisements, a TAA brochure on island holidays and the Sydney telephone directory. The choice is deliberately wide, and the material heterogeneous in the extreme. It is also cut up into segments varying from a few words to one and a half pages, and distributed throughout the text in serial fashion.[5] In practice, this is less confusing than might be supposed, since it is relatively easy to recognize most of the strands by their content and style.

On the other hand, the final major curiosity of "Letters from the Antipodes" is that not only is most of the text quoted, it is in a translated form which often pays little attention to accuracy. In the first place, Butor's translations are usually shorter than the original, whereas—because of its explicative nature—translation is normally inflationary.[6] The reductive nature of Butor's translation is mainly the result of generalized ellipsis: punctuation is frequently dropped, commas, colons or semi-colons replace full stops, main verbs frequently disappear, as do personal pronouns, the definite article and conjunctions. The combined effect of these alterations to the original is first, to create a notational style, and second, to strengthen the narrative qualities of the many white and Aboriginal legends reproduced.

The notational style may well owe something to the elliptical practices of journalism; for instance, newspaper headlines in French make frequent use of the colon in place of the verb.[7] It is most evident in certain strands of "Letters from the Antipodes" concerned with travel: those introduced by *Marie-Jo darling* or the extracts from Cook's Journal, which by their very nature already present this characteristic. Greater narrative coherence is achieved by considerable rewriting and, in the case of certain Aboriginal legends, by the actual conflation of myths.[8] There is also a certain stylistic variation, again in the case of Aboriginal legends, where an almost monotonous narrativity brought about by a series of clauses describing a series of successive actions and punctuated by commas (for example p.413) is occasionally disturbed by short sentences—one beginning with "And"—creating a solemn, quasi-Biblical effect quite absent from the original (p.404).[9] On the other hand, the extracts from French authors including Jules Verne are incorporated without modification, and the unique register of the massage parlour advertisements and the inflated banalities of the holiday brochures remain unaltered, in spite of alterations to punctuation and the suppression of verbs.

The text of "Letters from the Antipodes" thus betrays a series of tensions between the levelling force represented by generalized ellipsis, and the inbuilt stylistic resistance of material ranging from massage parlour advertisements to potted biographies in various works of reference, tensions that are complicated by attempts at stylistic variation in the Aboriginal legends. The present translation has attempted to maintain these tensions, as far as the innate differences between English and French allow.[10] Several months of struggling with Butor's text have brought me to the conclusion that translation is not impossible, as eminent thinkers such as Croce have claimed, but fraught with extraordinary difficulties of a largely semantic nature—what lies beneath the "lexical tip" of words, to use George Steiner's expression which makes Matthias Claudius's (untranslatable) assertion "Wer übersetzt, der untersetzt" particularly appropriate.[11]

The limits of translatability in the case of the present text will become apparent in the detailed discussion of Butor's aesthetic of juxtaposition (afterword), but one specific point might with advantage be mentioned now. If normal punctuation is systematically suppressed, it is partially replaced, as we have already seen, by "thematic punctuation" using the adjective "red" in "Letters from the Antipodes". In French, adjectives of colour almost invariably follow the nouns they qualify, agreeing with them in number and gender. In English there is no agreement, and they always precede the noun. This poses two difficulties, the first being that where "rouge" is used in its plural form in French (becoming "rouges") there is no change of textual strand, and because English makes no distinction between singular and plural in the case of adjectives, the reader may wrongly think in such cases that the word "red" indicates that he is passing from one strand to another. There seems no way around this problem; on the other hand, the difficulty posed by the different position of the adjective in English and in French is a more fruitful one, since what has been lost in the passage from French to English—the fact that "rouge" is at once a pointer to a change of strand and also a possible qualifier of a preceding noun (for example "désert rouge"/red desert)—is sometimes made up for if the *new* strand begins with a noun, which the punctuating adjective may similarly qualify. The effect may be totally different, but it is one of the encounters generated by Butor's framework and textual signposts.

A consideration of Butor's sources, and the transformations they have undergone, has proved to be a unique means of focusing on the text. But what the preceding discussion should not conceal is the fact that what follows is a translation of "Courrier des Antipodes"; it is *not* a reproduction of the sources which make up the bulk of the material. To have reproduced them in their original form would have been a means of pretending that "Courrier des Antipodes" did not exist, or at best of transforming it into an anthology. But if it is not an anthology, and given the heterogeneous nature of the material comprising it, what *is* the status of this extraordinary piece? For the interest of "Letters from the Antipodes" is not just that it is a text about Australia written by a Frenchman (indeed, this statement is far from accurate); it is also a work that obliges the reader to reconsider just about every aspect of the phenomenon of "literary activity". Its status, and that of its author, are among the many questions raised—and occasionally answered—in the afterword.

Notes

1. In the strand entitled *the ambiguous racism of Uncle Jules.*
2. Michel Butor, interview in *Meanjin*, 2 (1980), p.231.
3. *L'Emploi du temps* (*Passing Time*) and *La Modification* (*A Change of Heart*).
4. *Boomerang, le génie du lieu, 3* (Paris: Gallimard, 1978). The sections are broken up into blocks of between two and twelve pages and interwoven in a mathematically determined fashion (see afterword, section 2). The original pagination of "Letters from the Antipodes" has been kept as a reminder of how it is broken up in the French edition (numbering at top left and right of page), while the numbering at the bottom is regretfully necessary to convince booksellers that there are no missing pages . . .

5. See afterword, section 4.

6. George Steiner, *After Babel* (Oxford: Oxford University Press, 1975), p.227.

7. Groupe μ, *Rhétorique générale* (Paris: Larousse, 1970), p.87.

8. Compare "Letters from the Antipodes" pp. 371 and 381 with Butor's source, Charles Mountford, *Arnhem Land Art, Myth and Symbolism* (Melbourne: Melbourne University Press, 1956), pp. 323 and 325. Butor conflates three different extracts from Mountford in order to achieve an effect of dramatic contrast.

9. Mountford, p.218. For a similar example of stylistic variation, see translation, p.438 ("But the barramundi . . . then he tried to cut off his head . . . ").

10. See in particular J-P. Vinay and J. Darbelnet, *Stylistique comparée du français et de l'anglais* (Paris: Didier, 1968).

11. Steiner, *After Babel*, p.197. Claudius is quoted on p.269.

Letters from the Antipodes

at last a moment to write to you, Marie-Jo darling, I hope that Cécile got my telegram back home at The Antipodes and that she managed to send it on to you. There were no difficulties with my ticket at Nice; the only thing that worried the young lady was that the Sydney to Brisbane flight was on the seventh and I was leaving on the fifth, so she thought I was spending a night somewhere. As she couldn't quite believe me, she went and checked the timetable, and finally registered my case correctly. You won't have the same problem, since I'll make sure that I'm at Sydney airport to meet you. On the other hand, it's very likely that you'll have to pay extra since, following their usual practice, the airlines increased their fares by three per cent on July the first. I was on time at Rome airport; the terminal still isn't finished although it's been open for years, it's one of the most depressing places on earth, totally unworthy of the city and of its name, for it's called Leonardo da Vinci. At the transit desk (everybody there speaks French) they discovered that my ticket hadn't been made out properly. The Singapore Airlines London–Melbourne service via Amsterdam, Rome, Bahrain, Bangkok, Singapore and Sydney is a through flight, so that fortunately the luggage is not disturbed, but it is officially made up of two separate flights SQ712 and SQ712A which must be shown on two separate counterfoils forming part of the ticket. You give one up at Rome if you get on at Rome and the other as you go through transit at Singapore; in fact they use this to give you a new seat, which is sensible, for there are far less people on the second leg of the journey, so you can settle down more comfortably. Also, I had thought when I left Nice that there was only one means of getting to Brisbane by leaving on a Monday, but there are two flights from Nice to Rome almost at the same time and at least two Rome–Sydney via Singapore. I failed to check if you were on the same flight as me, since I took it for granted. Could you check your ticket for the flight numbers

AIR PUMP   (0 0)   OPOSSUM   (0 0)   PLASTIC   (0 0)   BIRD OF PARADISE go to the travel agent and sort it out for your peace of mind, and while you're there check all the travel times; send me all the details as soon as possible so that I can follow you in my thoughts *Marie-Jo darling* (0 0) LETTERS FROM THE ANTIPODES (0 0) *murmurs from Arnhem land* many spirits live in the surrounding countryside, say the people of Oenpelli, in clefts in the plateau, in waterholes on the plains, in termite mounds, hollow trees or caverns, but we never see them. Only the medicine-men of bygone days, sharper than those of today, sometimes glimpsed them. The most common are the harmless little mimi who made drawings on rock walls which were later often drawn over by our ancestors. They are so thin that they can only hunt in still weather, the least wind would break their frail bodies. They can hear and see much better than us, are more afraid of us than we are of them, and when they hear us coming they blow onto crevices in the cliffs to make them open for a moment so that they can find shelter. In the dreamtime a young girl engaged to an old relative came to detest him; she accepted the food he offered her and some-times came to sit in his camp during the day, but returned to her parents each sunset. In the end her father scolded her, saying: "that man is to be your hus-band, he feeds you, and yet when night comes you won't stay with him". Instead of replying she sat on the ground and wept copiously. In exasperation, her fiancé painted her image on the wall of a deep-seated cave and sang a song of such powerful magic over it that the girl fell so ill that her body died. Now, a harmless little mimi, she wanders among the rocks on the plateau red at all events, Marie-Jo darling, I had more than four hours to wait at Leonardo da Vinci airport. The plane arrived an hour late, so it didn't leave until shortly before midnight. Once I was settled there were of course no more problems; very pretty hostesses in blue batik dresses, charming stewards

ECHIDNA   (0 0)   STRAW   (0 0)   ALTAR   (0 0)   DRAGON LIZARD

4

before meals you're given a choice of champagne, beer and orange juice, during them Beaujolais or Graves, both excellent. The film started at one o'clock, but I fell asleep as soon as it began and didn't leave my seat at Bahrain as I wasn't properly awake *murmurs from Arnhem Land* (0 0) LETTERS FROM THE ANTIPODES (0 0) *bibliography of banknotes* on the front of the yellow, orange and sepia Australian dollar, the side with the signatures of the governor of the Australian reserve bank and the secretary to the treasury, next to the coat of arms flanked by the kangaroo and the emu, surmounted by the morning star on a background of waves, and divided into six compartments: top row, from left to right: NSW (New South Wales) with a cross studded with a star on each point, VIC (Victoria) with the constellation of the Southern Cross surmounted by the Queen's crown, QLD (Queensland) with the Maltese Cross, the Queen's crown in the centre; bottom row: SA (South Australia) with an eagle, WA (West Australia) with a black swan, TAS (Tasmania) with a lion that is also a wolf, a tiger and a demon (NT, Northern Territory, is missing, but there are so many Aborigines there, and ACT, Australian Capital Territory, but there are so many ambassadors there), the portrait of a still young woman with a slightly refractory expression, wavy hair, necklace, decorations, no identity given. The same on all the coins. In my search for sources of information in the library of the Queen's land university, I begin with the EB (Encyclopedia Britannica) 1968 edition: Queen of the United Kingdom of Great Britain and Northern Ireland, as well as other realms and territories, administratrix of the common wealth, born 21 April 1926 in Bruton Street, London, where her maternal grandparents, the Earl and Countess of Strathmore, then lived, and christened Elizabeth Alexandra Mary, eldest daughter of the Duke of York (later George VI), second son of King George V. The outbreak of the second world war meant parting from her parents. Lived with her sister, the Princess Margaret Rose, at Balmoral for the first few months, then at the Royal Lodge, Windsor, with occasional sojourns at the castle

BARK   (0 0)   GRAVING-TOOL   (0 0)   PLATYPUS   (0 0)   PAPER first broadcast made from there to evacuee children on 13 August 1940, first public appearance without her family in summer 1944 at a meeting of governors of the Queen Elizabeth Hospital for Children. Went with the King and Queen early in 1947 to South Africa where she celebrated her twenty-first birthday, speaking over the air to all who owed her suzerainty, and quoting the motto of many of her ancestors: "I serve", promising red it was a Boeing 747, Marie-Jo darling, I was lucky enough to be next to a window, kisses, but there was condensation between the two panes so that I could only see round the edges. As we left Bahrain I made out some oil wells. The daylight hours went by very quickly on Tuesday. I was wide awake at Bangkok, but transit passengers were not allowed to leave the plane for security reasons. At the previous stop there had been a procession of Arab cleaners, now there were Siamese cleaners. I saw a few rice fields. Everybody disembarked at Singapore. Crowds everywhere. Nobody speaks French. The shops are incredibly cheap, but it seems that they're even cheaper in the city where everything is duty free. I've got together quite a bit of information about the place, which sounds very strange. We could spend a day or two there on our way back to break the journey. So I got on the same plane again but in another seat with a completely transparent window. As the two seats next to mine were free I slept almost comfortably. Before dinner two singers serenaded us to the accompaniment of a guitar. Unfortunately they were American hits and poorly sung, but it's the first time that I've had such a treat in an aircraft. An excellent cognac after dinner, and like the day before I fell asleep at the beginning of the film red the harmless little mimi Mamgunmal and his family, say the people of Oenpelli, live in the rocks of the plateau; they only eat honey and the resin that oozes from the tree trunks

KEEL   (0 0)   LYRE-BIRD   (0 0)   WOOD   (0 0)   CENTAUR during the day the female sucks it from the bloodwood tree even though she knows it's for the males; so at night Mamgunmal spears her with his lance while she sleeps. As for the harmless little mimi Bumabuma, he lives a bachelor's life in a termite mound, he's very fond of honey, of hunting bandicoots, goannas and echidnas that he cooks over his fire *murmurs from Arnhem Land* (0 0) LETTERS FROM THE ANTIPODES (0 0) *red bicentenary dream* at nightfall in the streets of Flagstaff Arizona, an Indian from the Navajo or Hualapaï reserves, far away, I lean against a red brick wall among the garbage bins and newspapers in the light of neon signs and traffic, dreaming of fair-haired Floridan girls in their lagoons *red bicentenary dream* (0 0) LETTERS FROM THE ANTIPODES (0 0) *prelude to Cook* it was in 1519 that the Portuguese Ferdinand Magellan, commanding five Spanish vessels BOUGAINVILLE set out from Seville, discovered the strait that is named after him, through which he entered the Pacific where he discovered two tiny desert islands on the South side of the Line, then the Mariana Islands, and finally the Philippines. His vessel, named the Victory, and the only one of the five to return to Spain, via the Cape of Good Hope, was hoisted up onto land at Seville as a monument to that expedition, possibly the most daring that men had so far undertaken. Thus, for the first time, the spherical nature of the world and the extent of its circumference was demonstrated in a material manner. The Englishman Drake set out from Plymouth with five vessels on 15 September 1577, returning with only one on 3 November 1580. He was the second person to go round the globe. Queen Elizabeth came to dine on board, and his vessel, the Pelican, was carefully preserved in a dock at Deptford with an honourable inscription on its great mast red the mimi Bamunit and his wife live in the jungle near Kumada, say the people of Oenpelli, kisses, set traps for us if we venture onto their land where they spend most of their time hunting, but they don't eat the game they catch, they only live on raw yams, since they haven't yet discovered the secret of fire

KANGAROO   (0 0)   BRICK   (0 0)   CHAMELEON   (0 0)   EMU

I finally arrived at eleven. There was nobody to meet me. In any case, I had to wait for my bags to be unloaded. Then, after a few minutes, an announcement: "Would Mr Michel Butor please come to the information desk", where I met a young man who told me that there were some photographers and journalists in the press room; the university had told them I was coming. I asked them if there was anyone from there at the airport; they had no idea. They had MS's home telephone number, which I didn't have, and I rang him straight away. He was very surprised to hear me—he'd checked with Singapore Airlines that morning and they'd told him I wasn't on the flight. Do you remember that something similar happened in New Zealand five years ago—nobody to meet me at Wellington airport because the cultural attaché had rung Auckland and had been assured there was no Butor on the plane. My name is difficult to pick out for English ears. It's usually written Burton, like the novelist in *Passing Time*. I'd had a lot of trouble at Wellington, since the embassy was already shut, there was only a cleaning-woman and the attaché was at a reception where I finally managed to contact him through a babysitter. MS was dismayed, and told me he'd get his car straight away. Meanwhile the baggage had been unloaded, but my case wasn't with the rest. I had to fill in a form. They assured me that it would be on the next flight and would be sent to the French department *bibliography of banknotes* (0 0) LETTERS FROM THE ANTIPODES (0 0) *ghosts* in the Monaro region of NSW a black horse portending disasters has often been seen red at Brisbane airport, Marie-Jo darling, I finally went back to my journalists who were embarrassed because they couldn't do anything for me. Kisses. And so to the interviews and photographs (you can imagine how marvellous I felt). It was as if I was naked, with my raincoat in one hand and my typewriter in the other

DOVE   (0 0)   ECHIDNA   (0 0)   SILVER   (0 0)   SOUTHERN CROWN as for the giant Mikmik who lives in the jungle at the mouth of the river, he only eats fish red nothing on Elizabeth II in the DAB (Dictionary of Australian Biography), but three sections in the subject index, kisses: a) Queen of Great Britain: the Royal Visit and You, royal visit to Australia of Her Majesty Queen Elizabeth II and His Royal Highness the Duke of Edinburgh, 1954 compiled, photographed, written and designed by the Australian Bureau of Information, Department of the Interior, Canberra; Frank Benemy: The Queen reigns, she does not rule; Andrew Duncan: The Reality of Monarchy; Geoffrey Dutton: Australia and the Monarchy, a symposium . . . b) Art Collections, c) Coronation. Nothing in the author and title catalogue red before arriving at Sydney, Marie-Jo darling, you have to fill in two cards, one for the police, one for the customs and quarantine; the latter is in three languages: English, German and Croatian. You just have to put a cross in the boxes that show that you're as harmless as a mimi. You go through passport control, then wait for the luggage to come through for customs. I wasn't asked to open anything. I gave my case to the Australian airline with which I was flying to Brisbane. A charming hostess with Australian makeup—very blue eyelids, heavily-rouged cheeks—told me to leave it with her, she'd look after everything, and to take a bus to the domestic ter-minal. So I changed a few Swiss francs and made my way to the other building. I still had two hours to wait and it was quite chilly. I was barefoot in my sandals. I was sorry I hadn't opened my case at the customs for a pair of socks. Brilliant light—and me huddled in my raincoat. As it's all rather complicated, I'm going to arrange my trip to Sydney so that I can meet you; we'll start by spending a few days there, then we'll go to Brisbane together, it'll be much simpler and pleasanter

STONE   (o o)   COMPASS   (o o)   OPOSSUM   (o o)   COPPER this morning, the major national paper, the Australian, has a photograph specially featuring my feet in their sandals; they thanked me and left, and I remained alone in the lounge until MS arrived a few minutes later. He immediately reassured me about the bags—it seems that this kind of delay often occurs—and took me home for lunch red the English knight Thomas Cavendish, what are you doing Cécile, far away, set out from Plymouth on 21 July 1586 BOUGAINVILLE with three vessels, returning with two on 9 September 1588. This voyage, the third around the world, produced no discoveries. The Dutchman Oliver de Noort left Rotterdam on 2 July 1598 with four vessels, passed through the Strait of Magellan, ran along the West coast of America and thence on to the Marianas, the Philippines, the Spice Islands, the Cape of Good Hope, returning to Rotterdam with only one vessel on 26 August 1601. He made no discovery in the South Seas red the Munimunigan mimi lived among the great rocks of Unbalanja, say the people of Oenpelli, kisses, without axes for cutting down trees or getting honey from high up in the hives, spears to kill birds or animals, or fire to cook their food; during the wet season they suck the gum from eucalypts and sometimes find honey in abandoned termite mounds; during the dry season they have to live on acacia gum. They are very long haired. As for Noulabil, he lives with his wife and family in a large hollow tree at the base of the plateau and sets traps for us if we touch it. He lives in terror of Mamaragan the lightning man who travels in thunderstorms. At the first rumble he comes out of his tree, wiping the perspiration from beneath his arms and shouts to frighten the lightning spirit; who takes no notice, so that Noulabil and his family flee away into the caverns, while Mamaragan enjoys himself cutting down his tree with the stone axes that grow on his knees and elbows red on the back of the dollar note a White has utilized Aboriginal paintings, in particular those which the mimi painted in their likeness near Oenpelli.

DRAGON LIZARD   (0 0)   PEARL   (0 0)   CROW   (0 0)   PLATYPUS kangaroo hunt, collecting honey, and also those bark paintings that represent not only the outside but also the inside of creatures: a body stretched out, obviously a corpse, flanked by two figures squatting and singing as they strike two pieces of wood together, with a third one eating a kangaroo paw, surrounded by the other pieces of its body, numerous hives filled with honey, a large shade-tree, a large snake with two young, a male kangaroo hopping, and a goanna with its tongue hanging out. The article on Aborigines in the EB has this: the inhabitants found in a country at its first discovery. The Aborigines were a mythi-cal people of central Italy supposed to have descended from the region of Reate, an ancient Sabine town, upon Latium, whence they expelled the Siceli and settled down as Latini under a king Latinus. The etymology of the name ("ab origine") makes them the original inhabitants (Greek: autochthons) of the country, but is inconsistent with the fact that the oldest authorities (for example Cato in his Origines) regarded them as Hellenic immigrants and not as a native Italian people. Other explanations suggested are "arborigines" (tree-born) and "aber-rigines" (nomads). See Races of Mankind. Nothing of course in the DAB, but in the subject catalogue the cards are so numerous that I can only give the section headings: Aborigines—addresses, essays, lectures; amusements; anthropometry; antiquities; art; biographies; boats; social conditions; burials; Aboriginal children; their education; problems of Aboriginal citizenship; civil rights; civilization; craniology; culture; their history *bibliography of banknotes* (0 0) LETTERS FROM THE ANTIPODES (0 0) *reconnaissance* Monday 16 April 1770, fresh breezes at NNW with cloud and haze. In the afternoon we saw an egg-bird and yesterday a gannet COOK these are birds that never go far from land

CORAL   (0 0)   CUP   (0 0)   LYRE-BIRD   (0 0)   RUBY

Wednesday 18th, Southerly gale with violent squalls... Last night saw a Port Egmont hen and this morning two more, a speckled bird, several albatrosses and some black puffins, sure signs of the nearness of land red periòdicals on Aboriginal culture; dances; kisses; discography; illnesses; habitations; economic conditions; education; pre-school; primary; secondary; employment problems of Aborigines, general; in the NT; in QLD; statistics; exhibitions on red the German George Spilberg, what are you thinking about Agnès, in the service of Holland on the other side of the other end of the world without end, set sail from Zealand on 8 August 1614 BOUGAINVILLE with six ships, lost two vessels before he made for the Strait of Magellan, passed through it, privateered along the coasts of Peru and Mexico whence, without discovering anything on his way, he proceeded to the Marianas and the Spice Islands. Two of his vessels re-entered Dutch ports on 1 July 1617. At almost the same time James Lemaire and Schouten immortalized their names. They left Texel on 14 June 1615 with the vessels Concord and Horn, discovered the strait that bears the name of Lemaire, were the first to enter the South Seas by doubling Cape Horn, discovering at 15°15′S and around 142° from Paris the Isle of Dogs, at 15°S and 100 leagues to the West the Isle without Bottom, at 14°46′S and from 173 to 175°W of Paris two islands, the Cocos and the Traitors, 50 leagues further West the Isle of Hope, then the Isle of Horn at 14°56′S, around 179°W of Paris. Then they ran along the coast of New Guinea, passed between its western extremity and Gilolo and arrived at Batavia in October 1616. George Spilberg halted them there and sent them to Europe in vessels of the Company; Lemaire fell sick and died at Mauritius, Schouten returned to his native land; the Concord and the Horn returned two years and ten days later red the harmless little mimi Gadjimungaini is particularly hairy

SOUTHERN CROSS   (0 0)   KANGAROO   (0 0)   SAPPHIRE   (0 0)   SWORDFISH say the people of Oenpelli far away, he has no tools and has to live off the honey he finds in abandoned termite-mounds or clefts in the plateau, but it is he who invented all our hunting cries and vocabulary. As for the pitari, their bodies are covered with long hair similar to the dogs belonging to the White Man; like us they hunt kangaroos and wallabies red the inhabitants of Doonside on the outskirts of Sydney, kisses, were often aware of a convict and his friends haunting Bungaribee house built by Major John Campbell in 1876, right up until its demolition in 1957 red MS has a very nice house built on stumps as is usual here because of the floods, the insects and the heat (an Indonesian and SE Asian feature; some old buildings are quite Chinese-looking) but with some rooms downstairs including his study, Marie-Jo darling, and a garden filled with tropical plants; all the things that are sold in pots at home grow outside here—poinsettias, hibiscus, crotons, dracoenas . . . It's like being in a gigantic florist's shop. There's a very fine view of a hill covered with eucalypts, with houses at the bottom set above one another amidst palm trees. The weather's beautiful but decidedly cooler than it's been in Nice lately. It's cold enough for a pullover, especially in the morning and as soon as the Sun has set (it sets at its proper time here, which seems very early). After lunch my eyes began to blink. MS drove me to my college on campus. The university is on vacation until 19 July; so it's very quiet for the time being. I have a room divided into two—bedroom and study. A door opens onto a passage with toilet and shower, at the other end of which another one leads to the twin bedroom occupied by somebody else. You bolt your door when you've finished with the facilities. It's the system I once came across in the Saturn Club at Buffalo. During my four month stay there I never came across the "other person" *ghosts* (0 0) LETTERS FROM THE ANTIPODES (0 0) *documents* back home at The Antipodes I'm going through the things I brought back from my previous journey to the South Seas

EMU　　　(0 0)　　　GOLD　　　(0 0)　　　ERIDANUS　　　(0 0)　　　OPOSSUM

all that's most important is in two cardboard boxes. This Week in The Alice, 11 October 1971; Ansett Airlines of Australia knows a special Place for you, Central Australia 1971, the Big Country; Central Australian Tours Association; day tours from Alice Springs red for the moment I've a single bed, Marie-Jo darling, but they'll put a wider one or a second one in before you arrive, kisses; as it's midwinter here, I've been given three woollen blankets, and I needed them the first night, but tonight I think two will be enough. The only form of heating is a small electric radiator. MS has lent me a kettle, a cup and saucer etc., all I need to make breakfast. This morning I had breakfast in hall (there's an ecumenical conference or something similar on), but it's too noisy. Tomorrow I'll manage on my own. As you probably realize, as I'm using a typewriter, I've solved the problem of Australian power points; as usual it's with the help of the kettle lead; I'll buy two or three so that the appliances can all work at once. The prongs are flat, like in the United States, but there are always three to a plug and instead of being parallel they are in the form of a sort of little sheaf. As for the side you drive on, the girls were right and remembered better than I did what I'd said when I came back previously, it's on the left. Today I did various administrative things. I was introduced to various university officials. I have a library card, a bookshop credit card, I opened an account at the university branch of the Bank of NSW, and I had a look at the local shops, which are very badly off for postcards. I'll have to go as soon as possible to see what the city centre offers red yesterday afternoon fresh SSW breezes with cloud and a few squalls, what are you dreaming about Irène, at 5 a.m. reefed the mainsail

PLATINUM   (0 0)   FURNACE   (0 0)   ECHIDNA   (0 0)   DIAMOND and saw land extending from NE to West on the other side of the other end of the world. We continued steering to the Westward with the wind at SSW until eight o'clock COOK then made all sail and followed the coast to the NW . . . So far the land appears rather low and not very hilly, green and wooded, the seashore is all white sand. Friday 20th, the weather being clear enabled us to view this pleasant and promising country of moderate height with hills, slopes, plains and valleys with some grassland but mostly covered with forests; the slopes are gentle red in the dreamtime the harmless little dwarf mimi Dauandja who lived with his four wives, his son and his three daughters on the coast by the river mouth, say the people of Oenpelli on the other side of the other end of the world without end, made a bark canoe one day and set out with them for a distant island. Far out at sea a terrible storm claimed them. When Dauandja reached the bottom of the sea he declared: "here's a pleasant and promising spot; we'll each make separate camps and stay here, but before we do I'll send up a stream of fresh water so that my friends can quench their thirst if they're on long canoe journeys." And ever since then a fresh water spring has bubbled up right above their home and communicates with a sacred pool where only the elders may drink. Dauandja leaves it sometimes to catch crabs and fish from the swamps so as to vary his diet. As for the little mimi Guruwuldan he lives by himself near the Aruwatara swamp, hunting bush turkeys and Torres Strait pigeons that he cooks on his campfire red as for the people of Innamincka Crossing in the Centre, they hear the ghost of the explorer Burke far away groaning around the pub at night red fiction depicting Aborigines; food; kisses; games

CRANE   (O O)   DRAGON LIZARD   (O O)   OPAL   (O O)   CLOCK

Aboriginal health and hygiene; Aboriginal history; housing; implements; Aborigines in literature; in juvenile literature; children's novels about Aborigines red the Dutchman Jacques l'Hermite and Schapenham set out in 1623 with a fleet of 11 vessels BOUGAINVILLE with the project of conquering Peru; they entered the South Seas by Cape Horn and fought actions along the Spanish coastline whence they sailed to the Marianas without making any discovery in the South seas, then to Batavia. L'Hermite died as they left the Strait of Sonde, and his vessel, almost the only one remaining from his fleet, made land at Texel on 9 July 1626 *prelude to Cook* (0 0) LETTERS FROM THE ANTIPODES (0 0) *labels* as well as boomerangs decorated in various ways, pottery and kangaroo skins, the central Brisbane shop of the QLD Department of Aboriginals and Islanders Advancement sometimes sells precious objects with a guarantee of origin and bark paintings supplied by Arnhem Land missions. With a few exceptions, you can stick on their backs one of the 35 labels that partially explain them. The Lightning Woman: during the dry season, Bumerali lives in her sky home, but when the wet starts she leaves, carrying two long-handled stone axes, and travels in the thunderstorms, striking the ground, destroying the trees and terrifying the Aborigines. The bow at the top of the painting is a stormcloud; the wavy lines with circles at the end are the stone axes, and the central white band represents the lightning red in 1683 the Englishman Cawley set out from Virginia, kisses, doubled Cape Horn BOUGAINVILLE privateered along the Spanish coast, made for the Marianas and returned to England by the Cape of Good Hope, arriving on 12 October 1686. This navigator made no discovery in the South Seas; he claims that in the Northern Sea at 47°S and 80 leagues from the coast of Patagonia he discovered the Isle of Pepys. I have looked for it on three occasions and the English twice without finding it red the people of Dilga in the West of QLD hear the sound of a man dying, what are you reading Mathilde? It is, they think, the ghost of a certain Welford on the other side of the other end of the world without end, killed by Aborigines

PLATYPUS   (0 0)   CARBUNCLE   (0 0)   SEA SERPENT   (0 0)   LYRE-BIRD

16

red languages; laws concerning the Aborigines; legends; pictorial works representing them; missions to the Aborigines; mixed bloods; mortuary customs; museums devoted to the Aborigines; music; mythology red gentle breeze from the South and clear weather, we coasted along shore towards the North, far, far away. Yesterday afternoon we saw smoke on several occasions COOK a certain sign that there are inhabitants . . . On Sunday 22nd we steered along towards NNE with a gentle SW breeze and so close in that we could make out people on the beach. They appeared to be very dark or black, but I cannot say whether it was the colour of their skin or whether they were wearing clothes. At noon Cape Dromedary appeared at 28° South at a distance of 19 leagues. A remarkable peaked hill inland with its summit formed by what appeared to be a pigeon house (I have thus named it) appeared at North 32°30' West . . . The land near the coast continues to be of moderate height, forming alternately rocky points and sandy beaches, but inland between Mount Dromedary and Mount Pigeonhouse there are several quite high mountains; we were able to isolate only two, covered in trees, behind Mount Pigeonhouse, with remarkably flat summits and steep rocky cliffs all around them as far as we could see. The trees in this region seem to be tall and robust red in the dreamtime the harmless little Nalbidji mimi camped in forests and by rivers, hunting and fishing, say the people of Oenpelli at the end of the world, and if one of them happened to die, his relatives would place his body on a burial platform and leave it to decay for an indefinite time; one day their leader, seeing the skeletons turning into dust, decided to put things in order. He began by going to the nearby lagoon and spearing a bream with his lance so that they could eat it. He then taught his people a whole series of chants, showed the daughters of the dead man how to remove the dried body from its platform

ELIXIR   (0 0)   HYDRUS   (0 0)   KANGAROO   (0 0)   PLASTIC and their mother how to dismember it, clean all the bones, wrap them in paper-bark, and place them in a grotto where they would be sheltered from the rain. And he decreed that henceforth they would always act in the same way. Today they live under the rocks of Unbalanja in crevices that open when they breathe on them. They make fire to warm themselves by and to cook the kangaroos that the menfolk catch, the yams that their womenfolk dig up, but we never see any smoke. As for the Nadidjit they are fatter than the other mimi and cannot take refuge in the cracks into which most of the others slip; this is why they set traps for us if we disturb the game they track with the little black wallaroos they use as dogs red back home at The Antipodes I'm going through the contents of the first box: Tours in and around Alice Springs, kisses, the significance of Ayers Rock for Aborigines; Albert Namatjira's House; Shell map of the NT; Wildlife of the Centre; map of Central Australia, showing country seen and routes taken by some early explorers; the NT News for 4 October 1971; Programme of the Hermannsburg Aboriginal Choir Tour; label: Arnhemland Aboriginal Craft Token $6.50 red of course I wanted to write to you every day, Marie-Jo darling, until there would be no longer any likelihood of my letters arriving before you left, in other words at most until the 25th, and of course as you can already see that'll be quite impossible. So I'm taking advantage of this national general strike day called on account of the serious threat posed to social security by the Australian government to spend the after-noon going over everything before it gets too muddled: on Friday morning I was interviewed by two radio stations; for the second one, in town, MS ac-companied me. Afterwards we had a cup of tea in a snack bar, and then he drove me back to the university where two of his colleagues, one French and the other Australian, took me to lunch at the Faculty Club

INDIAN   (O O)   EMU   (O O)   STRAW   (O O)   HARE in the afternoon I set up a little exhibition of my books in the display windows at the entrance to the library. Of course I'm sorry that I couldn't bring more with me. Then MS took me to the city centre where I began to find my bearings. Virtually everything that's a little old, 50 years or more, is very English in style, but always painted in very bright colours; there are also some old colonial-style buildings, surrounded by balconies on every floor with wrought-iron balustrades, then there is a layer of American skyscrapers. Lots of covered arcades leading from one street to another with a mass of little shops. I looked for the department stores and only found them just before they closed at five o'clock; I returned by bus, which took a good half-hour. The city is traversed by the very winding Brisbane River, which is only crossed by a few bridges so that you sometimes have to make enormously roundabout journeys to get from one point to another. I was after a little radio and a pair of boots because of the danger of leeches on some of my explorations. So far I haven't been able to buy either *documents* (o o) LETTERS FROM THE ANTIPODES (o o) *the equivocal racism of Uncle Jules* in Captain Grant's Children: the reservation appeared to be completely abandoned. There was no trace of encampments or huts. The plains and areas of bush alternated VERNE and gradually the country took on a wild appearance. It appeared that no living being, man or beast, inhabited these remote parts until Robert, stopping at a clump of eucalypts, called out: an ape! an ape red on Saturday morning, Marie-Jo darling, MS took me home so that I could phone a professor in Adelaide to make final arrangements for my trip there, which will last from Wednesday afternoon to Monday morning (14 July dinner, a lecture in English and one in French, then the weekend in the mountains—I'll be glad to have boots), kisses, then I went off to explore an immense covered shopping centre nearby that can compare with the biggest we've ever seen in the United States. Once again, as all the shops shut at midday on Saturday, I didn't have the time to see or buy very much

OPOSSUM   (o o)   BARK   (o o)   WOLF   (o o)   ECHIDNA

I'm still setting up my little household. I borrowed an extra pillow from MS, I bought a teapot made in Taiwan, a little toaster, a tray with folding legs that can be used as a little table, a lamp so that I can read in bed at night and also work a little more comfortably at my desk. The sheets and towels are changed every Tuesday; there are washing and drying machines on the ground floor of the college's "Vatican" wing (it's an Anglican establishment, but the master is broadminded), operated by a slot-machine. I had lunch in college; it wasn't bad. In the afternoon I wanted to see how much time it would take to get to Indooroopilly Shoppingtown (closed); it took a good hour, it's easily five kilometers; the return journey took a good hour; I toasted several pieces of bread to make sure that my new acquisition was working properly, read a bit and went to the nearest shopping centre where I ate in a pizza restaurant run by a very friendly Italian. I located a Chinese restaurant in a basement, then I went to bed early because on Sunday we had agreed to start at five in the morning and go with a couple of young naturalists who are studying at the veterinary school to listen to the dawn chorus in the nearest national park red on the back of a bark painting: the Wandjina, inspired by extraordinary cave paintings in the Kimberleys described by Sir George Grey when he discovered them in 1837 as resembling human beings wearing long red robes like cassocks. What are you up to Cécile? The headdress or halo, as seen on sketches made by Grey, is decorated with a design which early linguists interpreted as an inscription in Sumatran or Malayan-Sumatran, in an alphabet of Red Sea merchants, or in Chaldaeo-Phoenician. Far, far away. The origin of the Wandjina is still a matter of debate, but recent research suggests that the halo round their heads is a headband as well as a symbolic representation of the rainbow-serpent

PAPER   (0 0)   TABLE MOUNTAIN   (0 0)   DRAGON LIZARD   (0 0)   WOOD the head itself, with its startling black eyes and its nose, is a representation of a human skull. There is no mouth. The radiating lines represent hair. The design in the centre of the chest is a pearl ornament and the vertical lines on the bodies, continuous or dotted, represent falling rain. The Wandjina do not talk and therefore have no need of a mouth; the Aborigines say that if they had one, it would rain so much that the whole world would be drowned red the harmless mimi Dignuk is tiny, say the people of Oenpelli at the end of the world, he wades through the marshes at night, catching fish with his bamboo lance and making a whistling noise. He sets traps for us when we make such a good catch that there's none left for his family with whom he lives beneath figtree roots on the edge of lagoons. His door is the same size as the entrance to a goanna's hole, and he has to enlarge it by blowing in order to get through. As for the timid Wiliwilia who lives a bachelor's life in the jungle by the river, he never eats fish red back home at The Antipodes I'm cataloguing the documents brought back from the South Seas in 1971 to the other end of the world. In the same box, another group bound with string: Shell Atlas of New Zealand; the New Zealand Heritage, numbers one and two with a Map; menu of the Skyline Room restaurant at Queenstown red Aboriginal antiquities from NSW on the other side of the other end of the vast world; origins of the Aborigines; periodicals published by Aborigines; paintings, illustrations representing the Aborigines; poetry of the Aborigines; portraits of Aborigines; psychology red clear serene weather. Yesterday afternoon had a light NNW breeze until 5 o'clock, then a calm on the other side of the end of the world without end. Saw several lots of smoke along the coast before nightfall, and two or three times a fire in the night. We lay becalmed until one o'clock in the morning, when we got a breeze from the land COOK at noon a little wind that veered to NNE

MICROSCOPE   (O O)   PLATYPUS   (O O)   BRICK   (O O)   FLY clear and pleasant weather. Yesterday afternoon we stood off shore until two o'clock, then tacked to bring us in until six, then tacked and stood off red the Englishman Wood Roger set out from Bristol on 2 August 1708, rounded Cape Horn, kisses, fought actions along the Spanish coast as far as California BOUGAINVILLE whence, by a route that was now well established, he proceeded to the Marianas, to the Spice Islands, to Batavia, and by doubling the Cape of Good Hope he made land at the Downs on 1 October 1711 red on 1 May 1956 the reverend R. S. C. Blance, an Anglican clergyman from Adelaide, took a photograph at Corroboree Rock, some 100 miles to the West of Alice Springs and the site of Arunta tribe initiation ceremonies. The developed picture showed the figure of a man in a kind of nightshirt, wearing a hat, with his hands clasped beneath his chin as if in prayer *ghosts* (0 0) LETTERS FROM THE ANTIPODES (0 0) *Australia unlimited* on the wall of my room in college: Australia and the Pacific, from the first daring canoe to the space capsules' splashdown, the Pacific has been one of the most exciting theatres of human endeavour. Australia, as part of a growing community of Oceanic nations, is playing its part in the modern Pacific concert. Map in the form of a circle cut off at the top and the bottom, surrounded by a brown and greenish-yellow frame. Broad transparent arrows show the major assumed migrations, arrowed lines the voyages of the principal explorers: Magellan 1519-21, Mendaña 1567-9, Quiros 1605-6, Tasman 1642-3, Cook 1769-70. In the centre, marked by black dots, the international date line. An enormous red hibiscus, the flower of the Pacific, partly hides North America red the inhabitants of the port of Broome WA see the Roebuck sailing by, kisses, the phantom vessel of William Dampier who feared neither the devil nor the deep sea red the ship being no more than two miles from the shore, Mr Banks, Dr Solander, Tupia and myself went in the yawl to land at a spot where we had seen four or five natives who fled into the woods as we approached; what are you eating Agnès? we were disappointed at not being able to observe them at close quarters or even to speak to them

LYRE-BIRD   (0 0)   STONE   (0 0)   LEVEL   (0 0)   KANGAROO but above all because we were not able to land by reason of the surf beating the whole length of the shore on the other side of the other end of the world. In the woods were various palms and no undergrowth; it was all we could make out from the boat, after which we returned to the ship around five o'clock in the afternoon COOK at dawn this morning we discovered a bay that appeared fairly well sheltered from the winds, and I decided to enter it with the ship, which is why I sent the quartermaster in the pinnace to sound the entrance while we kept tacking. Sunday 29th, in the clear afternoon weather, Southerly winds with which we entered the bay and anchored in six fathoms near the southern shore around two miles from the entrance. Saw on both sides of the bay as we came in several natives and some huts. Men, women and children on the southern shore opposite the ship; landed in the boats in the hope of speaking with them, accompanied by Mr Banks, Dr Solander and Tupia; as we approached they all fled except for two men who seemed determined to prevent us landing. At once I ordered the boats to stop in order to speak to them, but this was to little purpose since neither we nor Tupia understood one word they said. So we then threw some nails, beads etc. ashore; they took them and did not seem too displeased so I thought they were inviting us to land; but I was mistaken, for as soon as we tried they again began to oppose us, whereupon I discharged a musket among them, which had no other effect than to make them retreat to where they had a stock of javelins, and one of them took up a stone and threw it at us, which made me fire a second musket loaded with small shot, and although some of the shot must have struck the man it had no other effect than to make him lay hold of a sort of shield to defend himself

COPPER   (0 0)   OCTANT   (0 0)   EMU   (0 0)   SILVER red ten years after Wood Roger, the Mecklemburger Roggeveen in the service of Holland on the other side of the other end of the world without end, set out from Texel with three vessels BOUGAINVILLE entered the South Seas by Cape Horn, where he looked for Davis Land without finding it, discovered Easter Island to the South of the Tropic of Capricorn at an undetermined latitude, then the Pernicious Islands between the 15th and 16th parallel south where he lost one of his vessels; then about the same latitude the Aurora and Vesper Islands, the Labyrinth made up of six islands, and Recreation Island where he put in. He then discovered below the 12th parallel south three islands that he named the Bauman's Isles, and finally below the 11th parallel south the islands of Tienhoven and Groningen; working along New Guinea and Papua, he landed at Batavia where his vessels were confiscated. Admiral Roggeveen himself returned to Holland on the vessels of the Company, and reached Texel on 11 July 1723, 680 days after his departure from the same place red back home at The Antipodes the Armidale Express and New England General Advertiser of 25 May 1870 relating the arrest of the bandit Thunderbolt, reproduced as a supplement to the Armidale Express and Uralla Times of 20–21 May 1970, far away; programme of MB's lecture tour of Australia; Shell Touring Guide to Sydney and environs; cutting from the Sydney Herald of 25 September '71: loneliness ends tribe's desert life; Australian Aboriginal Culture, an exhibition arranged by the Australian National Committee for UNESCO in 1953; D. Baglin and B. Mullins, Captain Cook's Australia with excerpts from his diary; copy on a sheet of writing paper from the Whitehall Hotel overlooking Sydney harbour of page nine of the city's telephone directory red

PEACOCK   (O O)   OPOSSUM   (O O)   BEAD   (O O)   PHOENIX rehabilitation of Aborigines; religions; rites; semiology; social conditions; social life; dictionaries; song red on the back of a bark painting: the Lightning brothers, these three human- and gecko-like beings are associated with rain; the Aborigines believe that the lightning brothers live in a cave during the wet season and spend the rest of the year travelling from place to place at the end of the vast world. Yagtchadbulla is the biggest. His splendid head-dress consists of a large white circle from which radiate 31 black and white lines. The two brothers have large black eyes, but no mouth or nose. They are outlined in white, have been circumcised and subincised, but only the youngest, Tcabuinji, is married; his wife Kananda is seen under his arm, represented by a black oval that is her body; the upper two projections are her ears, and the red shape her vulva; her entire figure is outlined in yellow red the harmless little mimi Naluk only eats yams, say the people of Oenpelli at the other end of the world. As for Timara, in the dreamtime he caught a great catfish at Kurultul near the mouth of the river, put it on his shoulders and went into the jungle until he reached Gugandja which he found so much to his liking that he decided to become its little mimi and settle there permanently; he sleeps in a deep grotto whose entrance is a cleft in a large hollow tree red and he pointed out a big black body which, gliding from branch to branch with surprising agility, went from treetop to treetop, kisses, as if it were kept in the air by some kind of membranous device VERNE so in this strange country apes flew like those foxes to whom nature has given bats' wings red I wound up the alarm I'd been lent, Marie-Jo darling, but I was woken well before four by some student noise, no doubt the dying embers of the ecumenical congress. So I had a first breakfast, then I put on the warmest things I had; MS lent me an extra sweater and we set off for the mountains. On the way we came across some rat kangaroos and some pademelons, very pretty little kangaroos the size of a large cat

ECHIDNA   (0 0)   CORAL   (0 0)   PAINTER   (0 0)   DRAGON-LIZARD

the Sun was already up when we reached the very spectacular subtropical rain-
forest with its abundance of birdsong. We had a second breakfast towards eight
o'clock, our teeth chattering because of the cold, then lunch towards midday.
The weather was fairly unpleasant, with a drizzle, but the temperature had
climbed considerably since dawn. I was lucky enough to see for the first time
a bower, that is, the edifice built by the satin bower bird. In order to court
the female, he builds a kind of avenue of twigs (about 20 cm high by 30 long;
the two walls are 10 apart) surrounded by a terrace covered with dead leaves,
various bits of rubbish, and above all decorated by anything he can find in
a brilliant blue; for instance there were some broken biros and various other
objects made of plastic or glass. Apparently later on he will dye the inside of
his avenue blue; formerly he used the juice of certain berries, but now, at least
in this region, they go and steal washing powder. We waited for a while but
he didn't condescend to show himself *the equivocal racism of Uncle Jules* (0 0)
LETTERS FROM THE ANTIPODES (0 0) *the groves of death* when one of us dies,
says the people of Yirrkala, his relatives gather round his dead body, wailing
with all their might, the women cut their scalps with sharpened bones until
the blood flows red the satin bower bird is apparently dark blue, Marie-Jo darling; another species speckled with yellow goes after yellow, kisses, another goes
after what shines; the most extraordinary edifices are constructed by a species
in New Guinea. They are not nests, but gardens of seduction; the nest itself
is constructed in the treetops by the female who has succumbed. We also saw
a scrub turkey's mound, made of dead leaves, a metre high. When fermentation
has raised the inside temperature of the mass sufficiently for incubation to occur
the female comes to lay her eggs. From now on, the male spends his time remov-
ing or replacing leaves to stablize the inside temperature which varies no more
than one degree. When the young hatch they are sufficiently mature to dig
their own tunnel and reach the air; the mound is abandoned and everything
begins all over again somewhere else

RUBY   (0 0)   SOUTHERN FISH   (0 0)   PLATYPUS   (0 0)   SAPPHIRE red further round the map where are you Irène, on the wall of my room in college: seascape at Sunset at the end of the world, violet clouds, a canoe with a triangular sail, in the distance what is probably the shore of an island. The first Australians and Melanesians came from SE Asia when, during the last ice age, much of the seabed to the North of Australia had emerged, with New Guinea forming part of the same continent. This discovery of land to the South of Asia was possibly made by fishermen lost at sea in their primitive craft. After the accidental landfalls, there were probably planned voyages of migration red the harmless little mimi Gradau is covered in hair, say the people of Oenpelli at the other end of the world, one day he threw his lance at a wallaby so hard that it flew away and is still flying. As for Naljanio, he isn't speedy enough; one day when he was hunting he tried to flee from a storm, but he was soaked to his thin bones before he could reach his crevice; he has streamed with water ever since red meanwhile the wagon had stopped and everyone followed the progress of the animal which gradually disappeared among the tops of the eucalypts on the other side of the other end of the dazzling world. Soon they saw it come down again at lightning speed VERNE run along the ground with countless contortions and leaps, then seize with its long arms the smooth trunk of an enormous gum tree. They wondered how it would get up the slippery, straight tree around which it could not get its arms. But the ape made little staggered notches in the trunk with a kind of axe and, by means of these regularly-spaced holds, he reached the fork of the gum tree. In a few seconds he had disappeared amongst the foliage red Aboriginal sport; teaching; red on the back of a bark painting a pregnant woman: she is with a jabiru bird, and the stings of a poisonous ray project from many parts of her body, far away

STERN   (0 0)   LYRE-BIRD   (0 0)   GOLD   (0 0)   COMPASS

Aranga: this evil spirit is portrayed with a rainbow serpent's head and his elbows
are decorated with ornaments. Dijalmung: the big-eyed owl sang so well one
day that Dijalmung the snake-spirit began to dance. He has the body and head
of a snake, arms and legs like a human; he holds a long stick in one hand
as he dances round a grave, which, through mission influence, is surmounted
by a cross red the fashion for great voyages seemed entirely dead when in 1741
Admiral Anson, far, far away, made his voyage round the globe BOUGAIN-
VILLE the excellent account of which is in everybody's hands, and which added
nothing to geography red back home at The Antipodes I'm still going through
the contents of the second box: in another group of papers Shell map of VIC;
T. Jones, Arnhem Land music; the Melbourne Planetarium; a series of cuttings
from the 20–23 September '71 Melbourne Age concerning the health of Aborigines at Alice Springs red the people of Broome WA also tell how the Anglican
Bishop Gerard Trower, while in residence at the bungalow known today as the
Bishop's Palace, kisses, awoke one night with the chilling feeling that someone
was watching him. "Who's there?" No reply. He called again, thinking that one
of his parishioners might be wanting him; silence. Then a ghostly figure moved
out of the shadows into the Moonlight. The strange visitor wore the robes of
a rabbi. He lingered an instant, then disappeared. When in the morning the
bishop attempted to describe him, his parishioners recognized a pearl-buyer
named Davis who had once lived in the bungalow as the heart and soul of
the Jewish community and had disappeared in a shipwreck red last night seaman
Torby Sutherland departed this life and tonight we buried his body on the shore
by the watering place; and I gave his name to the southern tip of this bay.
We found two sorts of gum COOK one of which is like gum dragon and is
identical, I think, to what Tasman took for gum lac; it oozes from the biggest
tree in the woods *reconnaissance* (0 0) LETTERS FROM THE ANTIPODES (0 0)
Unesco exhibition who are the Aborigines? A people of medium stature with
slender limbs

KANGAROO   (0 0)   PLATINUM   (0 0)   NET   (0 0)   EMU wavy hair, heavy eyebrows, deep-set brown eyes, wide nostrils, thick lips and a long head. The lower part of face protrudes markedly. Some believe that one race alone inhabits the continent, others that there are three main physical types: the first, related to Negrito stock, with frizzly hair, which was partly eliminated by two strictly Australian strains, stout and hairy-bodied in the South, and dark with sparse hair in the north. The Tasmanians were a Negrito type, of medium stature, with a broad nose, thick lips, prominent eyebrows, medium facial protrusion and a rounded head. They reddened their frizzly black hair with ochre red the great quantity of unknown plants, etc. which Mr Banks and Dr Solander collected in this bay made me name it Botany Bay. It is situated at 34°S and 208°37′W; kisses; it is vast, safe and convenient; it can be recognized by the even and moderately high nature of its shore, rather higher than it is inland, with steep rocky cliffs at the sea's edge, and it looks like a long island lying along the coast; the entrance to the port lies about the middle of this land; coming from the South, you sight it before you are abreast of it, which is not possible coming from the North; this entrance is scarcely more than a mile across and lies WNW. To enter it you must follow the southern shore to a little bare island which is close to the north shore COOK the country is flat and covered with low lying forests for as far as we can see into the interior, and I believe that the soil is generally sandy. In the woods there is a great abundance and variety of birds such as cockatoos, lorikeets, parrots, etc. and crows exactly like those we have in England. A lot of waterfowl at the entrance to the port where there are large flats of sand and mud on which they seek their food, most of which is unknown to us. On the sand and mud banks there are oysters, mussels, cockles, etc. which must be the main sustenance of the inhabitants who go at low water in their little canoes and pick them out of the sand or mud with their hands and sometimes cook and eat them in their boats where they often have a fire for that purpose

DIAMOND   (0 0)   SCULPTOR   (0 0)   OPOSSUM   (0 0)   OPAL the Natives do not seem very numerous and do not form large groups, but are scattered along the shore; those I have seen were about the same stature as Europeans, very dark in colour, but not black, and with hair that is not woolly and frizzly, but black and lank like ours. They had neither clothing nor ornament, and we have never seen any in their huts, from which I conclude that they never wear any ... However we know virtually nothing of their customs, for we have not succeeded in entering into relations with them; they scarcely touched the objects we left for them in their dwellings ... From what I have said of the natives of New Holland, they may appear to be the most wretched people on earth, but in reality they are far happier than we Europeans; being unaware not only of the superfluous commodities but also of those which seem to us to be necessary and which are so sought after in Europe, they are happy in not knowing the use of them. They live in a state of tranquillity untroubled by inequality of condition: the earth and the sea of their own accord provide all that is indispensable, they desire neither magnificent houses, furniture, etc., living in a warm and beautiful climate and enjoying a very healthy air, so that they have very little need of clothing and appear perfectly aware of this for many of them to whom we gave pieces of cloth left them carelessly on the shore or in the woods, having no use for them. In short they seem to have set no value on what we have given them, and did not wish to part with any of their articles in exchange for ours; which shows to my way of thinking that they consider themselves provided with all the necessities of life and that they have nothing superfluous. During our stay in this port, I had the English colours displayed ashore every day and an inscription engraved on a tree near our watering place with the ship's name, the date, etc. Having seen everything there was in this place, we left in the morning with a light breeze from the NW

SHIELD   (0 0)   ECHIDNA   (0 0)   CARBUNCLE   (0 0)   TELESCOPE and the wind soon after veering to the South we followed the coast towards NNE and at noon we were at latitude 33°50′S about three miles from land and abreast of a bay or port where there appeared to be a good anchorage and which I called Port Jackson red back home at The Antipodes This Fortnight in Tas 8–21 October '71; what are you dreaming about Mathilde? This Week in Adelaide 8–14 October '71; tourist map of Perth; Fremantle museum WA red the people of Devlin's Pound WA tell how the enormous Irish wine merchant who gave his name to the locality used to sneak cattle or sheep while the drovers got drunk in his establishment at the end of the dazzling world and that, mounted on a white horse, he drives his ghostly beasts red on the back of a bark painting: Malay boat: for many years, possibly centuries, Malay fishermen left Indonesia and, carried by the NW monsoon winds, reached Australia at the other end of the world, establishing their camps on the coasts of Groote Eylandt and Arnhem Land. During the wet season, helped by the Aborigines, they collected trepang, an edible holothurian, and pearlshell from the coral reefs. When the SE winds of the dry season started to blow, they returned home with laden boats. The wooden hull is divided into holds in which the produce is stowed. Above is a bamboo cabin; the difference in material can be seen. The mast has two stays that make it look like a tripod, the sail is made of matting. Two bumpers and a bowsprit complete the picture. The curved white lines projecting from the prow and the stem are the wake red after the voyage of Admiral Anson no other important ones were made for more than 20 years on the other side of the other end of the world. The spirit of discovery has recently seemed to be reawakened BOUGAINVILLE Commodore Byron set out from the Downs on 20 June 1764, went through the strait of Magellan, discovered a few islands in the South Seas, steering NW, reached Batavia on 28 November 1765, Cape Town on 24 February 1766, and on the ninth of May the Downs

DRAGON LIZARD   (O O)   ELIXIR   (O O)   TRIANGLE   (O O)   PLATYPUS

31

688 days after his departure red what on earth's that ape? asked the major. That ape on the other side of the other end of the red world without end, replied Paganel VERNE is a pure-blooded Australian red further round the map, on the wall of my room in college: excavations at Lake Mungo far, far away in NSW have shown that the Aborigines were living there about 40,000 years ago. They probably entered the continent by what is now the NW, while the Melanesians reached what later became the island of New Guinea. 6,000 years ago agriculture as practised by the tribes of SE Asia related to the Malays began filtering into New Guinea, and 5,000 years ago the farmers themselves slowly began moving in their seagoing boats through the Indonesian archipelago towards that island, to which they brought a neolithic culture red the harmless little mimi Makurindba lives with his wife and three children in a gorge between two pillars and feeds his family on yams alone, say the people of Oenpelli at the end of the world; as for the terrible mamandi Warluk, he lives with his wife and family in a land we cannot see beyond the clouds. He descends to Earth to look for acacia gum, fish that he catches with his bare hands and hives of wild bees in abandoned termite mounds. He doesn't know how to make fire, but comes into our camps at night and steals cooked portions of kangaroo or fish which we have left on the branches for the next day, and even the splashes of fat on the ashes. From time to time he'll come and settle down near us, and if we get too near to his camp, he is quite capable of projecting one of his own bones into our body; one of our medicine-men then has to extract it magically by the power of his song, otherwise we die slowly red when one of us dies, the men gather, say the people of Yirrkala, kisses, and sing the hymns and lays of his group red this morning I was to call on the university's vice-chancellor (rector) again, Marie-Jo darling, but he's also on strike, and as I already paid my respects last Thursday, I hope that'll be enough

PLASTIC   (0 0)   TOUCAN   (0 0)   LYRE-BIRD   (0 0)   STRAW

I went to check that the buses weren't running, then I browsed in the library and bookshop which had remained open. I got caught in a heavy shower; I lunched in the students' union which will be closed this evening. I'm not too sure where I'll manage to eat if I can avoid college, but it doesn't really matter since MS is putting on a wine and cheese party at home to introduce me to those members of his department whom I haven't yet met. Tomorrow morning I'll go into town to buy my boots. In the afternoon I leave for Adelaide. I'll return on the Monday morning which is when courses begin. By then they'll certainly have my seminar times arranged. I leave again on 3 August for Sydney so that I can meet you at the airport on the morning of the 4th. We'll be staying with friends. We'll stay there until the end of the week so that you can recover and have a look round Sydney which I like very much, then they'll drive us to Brisbane which we'll reach on Sunday evening after an overnight on the way *the groves of death* (o o) LETTERS FROM THE ANTIPODES (o o) *red archipelago dream* I go with a friend and his wife to meet you at Sydney airport. I think you're arriving on the Singapore Airlines flight, but I know that about the same time an Alitalia and a KLM plane coming from the same place are also due to land. It's very cold. It's six o'clock in the morning, but it is still pitch red. The gates out of customs are so arranged that it's impossible to catch sight of passengers before they finally come out. Red Australians returning from just about everywhere, especially Europe, begin to come through, laden with souvenirs, and red hordes of Japanese tourists. On the arrival board an indefinite delay for Alitalia is shown. Day is breaking. The last red passengers come out. You aren't there *red archipelago dream* (o o) LETTERS FROM THE ANTIPODES (o o) *small ads* in the Adelaide Advertiser for Monday 19 July '76: Angelique's friendly massage

SAILS   (o o)   KANGAROO   (o o)   BARK   (o o)   FLYING FISH

Abigail's warm massage red no doubt you're wondering, Marie-Jo darling, why I'm using a typewriter to write to you, kisses, which is something I never do. It's because I want to keep a copy of what I've written to you so that I can check it; these letters form a kind of travel diary which, as you've already guessed, I intend to use, with many cuts and alterations, for the book I'm working on. This is as you know the third volume of The Spirit of the Place which is to be called Boomerang (the shortest way between my room and the little shopping centre is via Boomerang Road). The only part that is so far written is the text of the catalogue of Bicentenary Kit, which will naturally have to undergo a certain number of alterations red where do the Aborigines come from? What are you reading Cécile? It is generally believed to be from SE Asia, far, far away. Some believe that the Tasmanians once inhabited the Australian continent and that they crossed Bass Strait either when it was still dry, a very long time ago, or by canoe red the terrible Namarakain mamandi are as thin as the mimi, say the people of Oenpelli at the end of the world, they steal the spirit of the sick by extracting it from the solar plexus, cook and eat it. Our medicine-men know how to ferret them out and spear them. They have big ears which enable them to hear much better than us, play perpetually with string which helps them to move among the trees, rocks and clouds. As for the terrible mamandi Garkain, he lives a bachelor's life in thick jungle near the river mouth. If someone crosses his domain, he flies up and bears down on him, enveloping him in the great folds of his skin which act as wings or fins. He sleeps in the daytime under a pile of leaves, hunts at night and eats his victims raw red when one of dies

EMU   (O O)   PAPER   (O O)   EUCALYPTUS   (O O)   AIR PUMP the next morning his body is rubbed with red ochre, say the people of Yirrkala at the other end of the red world, upon which his totemic design is painted red further round the map on the wall of my room in college: while the Australian Aborigines were refining their hunting skills and their arts (painting, singing, dancing—illustrations) on the other side of the other end of the world without end the Melanesians of New Guinea developed their agriculture. The Asian colonists brought with them certain plants like the yam and the taro which the New Guineans still cultivate today (the main Highland crop, the sweet potato, is of South American origin). New Guinea is one of the few places in the Pacific where the art of pottery has survived the lack of clay and the ready supply of coconuts and shells for containers. The art of the coast-dwellers includes a great variety of painting and sculpture often carried out on everyday things such as arms and cooking utensils. The art of the mountains consists almost entirely of body decoration. It was the arrival of the Indonesians on the islands to the NW of Australia that forced the Melanesians to emigrate to the East, thus populating the Solomons, the New Hebrides, Fiji and New Caledonia red two months after Commodore Byron's return, Captain Wallis, far away, set out from England with the vessels Dolphin and Swallow BOUGAINVILLE went through the Strait of Magellan, became separated from the Swallow commanded by Captain Carteret as he disembogued into the South Seas; there he discovered an island near the 18th parallel around August 1767, sailed back up to the Line, passed between the islands of Papua, reached Batavia in January 1768, put in to the Cape of Good Hope, and finally returned to England in the month of May of the same year red it was a depressing sight. About ten tents stood on the bare earth. These "gunyahs" made out of overlappingstrips of bark-like tiles, protected their miserable inhabitants on one side only VERNE these beings degraded by poverty were repulsive

OPOSSUM   (O O)   SOUTH   (O O)   WOOD   (O O)   WATTLE there were about thirty of them, men, women and children, dressed in tattered kangaroo skins resembling rags. Their first movement, as the wagon drew near, was to flee. But some words pronounced in an unintelligible patois by Ayrton appeared to reassure them. They came back then, half trustful, half fearful, like animals tempted by some tasty morsel red Frederick Fisher, a freed convict at the end of the red world, disappeared from his little hut in mid-1826, say the people of Campbelltown NSW. His companion George Worrall told his neighbours that Frederick had returned to England with no hope of returning and had left him his belongings. But a certain Farley was driving across a bridge one evening in October 1826 when he thought he saw Fisher sitting on the railing and reported the matter to the police; in daylight they discovered blood-stains on the spot where the ghost had been sitting. They fetched a black tracker who searched the bed of the creek beneath it and announced that he smelt white man's fat. They discovered Fisher's body at the bottom of a pool and Worrall was hanged on 5 February 1827 red Milky Way (on the back of a bark painting): two brothers lost their lives while travelling in a canoe; their bodies, in the central panel at the other end of the world, became the dark parts of the Milky Way in our constellations of Serpent and Sagittarius, and the canoe a line of four stars near Antares. The wavy pattern on the two outer panels represents the wake of the travellers' boat; they are the luminous parts of the Milky Way near our Scorpio. Upper panel: the elder brother standing on the rock on which he landed, indicated by a black area, part of the Milky Way near Theta Serpentis red at noon I observed that we were at 32°53′S and 208°W, kisses, about two leagues from the land which extended from N41°E to S41° COOK a small round rock or island near the shore red back home at The Antipodes I'm going through the things I brought back from my first journey to Australia in 1968: a bark painting representing a turtle

BIRD OF PARADISE   (0 0)   ECHIDNA   (0 0)   WESTERN   (0 0)   BRICK

a kangaroo fur cardigan for Marie-Jo, a toy koala for Mathilde *documents* (o o)
LETTERS FROM THE ANTIPODES (o o) *islands in the Sun* do you remember the
good old days? Those holidays you hoped would never end? Do you spend
your evenings looking at old photos that bring back fond memories? Yes, we
believe in the good old days, and our islands in the Sun will bring them back
to you in the form of new memories: white sandy beaches, clear blue ocean,
endless sunshine, where tranquil days pass slowly and leisurely red back home
at The Antipodes I'm going through the things brought back from my second
journey to Australia: an X-ray style bark painting representing a barramundi,
a wooden man with a loincloth made of string and feathers, kisses, a bird, a
wooden goanna, a green glass lance-tip fixed to part of a wooden haft red Orion
and the Pleiades on the back of a bark painting: from a country situated east
of Arnhem Land two canoes, one full of men, the other of women, were
approaching Yirrkala, Agnès, what are you doing? The men speared a turtle
at the end of the world, the women caught two fish. Near Cape Arnhem to
the East of Yirrkala the two canoes were swamped in a storm and all their
occupants were drowned. The men, the women, the turtle, the two fish and
a whale that happened to be in the vicinity (shown on the right) were transformed into stars which are visible during the wet season. The T-shaped object
in the upper left-hand corner represents the canoe carrying the men who are
the black dots above, forming the constellation we now call Orion. The rectangular area with dots below is the women's canoe, our Pleiades. The two fishes,
the turtle and the whale are parts of the Milky Way. The whole remaining
area is decorated with cross-hatched lines; those near the whale represent his
wake, the others the stormy waves red Southerly winds at day and a gentle
Westerly breeze and clear weather at night COOK saw several lots of smoke
on the inland plains

BANKSIA   (o o)   ALTAR   (o o)   DRAGON LIZARD   (o o)   NEW SOUTH WALES from this I concluded that there were lagoons where the natives found their subsistence red the natives, who were between five feet four and five feet seven inches tall, had a dusky complexion, not black, but the colour of old soot, fleecy hair, long arms, a prominent belly, on the other side of the other end of the inverted world, a hairy body scarred by tattooing or by incisions made during tribal ceremonies VERNE nothing could be quite as horrible as their monstrous form, their enormous mouth, their nose flattened against their cheeks, their protuberant jaws armed with white but proclivous teeth. Never had human beings so clearly exhibited animal traits red Fedirici, the famous Italian bass, was playing Mephistopheles in Gounod's Faust at the Princess Theatre, say the people of Melbourne on the other side of the other end of the world without end. Just as he was about to disappear in a cloud of sulphurous smoke, he slipped on the edge of the trapdoor, broke his spine, and died backstage. To this day, he can be seen in evening dress walking amongst the empty seats after the performance red except in New Caledonia where the mining and smelting of nickel have become the main industries, most Melanesians retain their agricultural way of life. They live in small communities which, in order to prevent too frequent wars, far away, have developed systems of ceremonial exchange red after having undergone many hardships in the South Seas, far, far away, Carteret reached Macassar in the month of March 1768 BOUGAINVILLE with the loss of nearly all his crew, Batavia on 15 September, the Cape of Good Hope at the end of December

STONE   (O O)   CLIANTHUS   (O O)   GRAVING-TOOL   (O O)   PLATYPUS it will be seen that I met him at sea on 18 February 1769 about 11°N. He did not reach England until the month of June red when one of us dies two bark effigies are made and slipped under his arms, say the people of Yirrkala at the end of the world, and he is told that they are his children who have been killed and placed next to him so that he should not feel too lonely and desire to return and haunt the living red on the front of the black green and yellow with a touch of orange $A2 note: next to a superb merino sheep framed by a ribbon at the other end of the inverted world, a man with a fancy cravat: MacArthur. The EB has nothing on him. DAB: John (1767–1834), pioneer and founder of the wool industry, born near Plymouth, Devon. His father Alexander had fought for Prince Charles Edward in 1745, and after Culloden had fled to the West Indies. Some years later, on his return to Plymouth, he established a business there. His son was educated at an exclusive school and entered the army in 1782 as an ensign, but having been placed on half pay in 1783 he went to study law at Holsworthy, Devon, but in 1788 he was in the army again and married Elizabeth Veale, the daughter of a country gentleman. In June 1789 he was appointed a lieutenant in the NSW Corps, sailed from Plymouth for Australia with his wife and son on 14 November 1789 in the Neptune, and immediately quarrelled with the captain with whom he fought a duel without serious consequences. After a long and trying voyage the Neptune arrived at Port Jackson on 28 June 1790 red what are their tribal territories? 680 tribes each of 200 to 700 people have been recorded on the other side of the other end of the world. Each of these occupied a separate territory. Today tribal life is preserved only in remote parts of Cape York, the NT, Central Australia and WA. There were about 275,000 Aborigines in Australia in 1778 when white settlement began; today there remain 30,000 full-bloods and 50,000 mixed bloods

QUEENSLAND (0 0) COPPER (0 0) HAKEA (0 0) KEEL

in Arnhem Land the tribes consist of totemic clans, each containing several linguistic groups red the terrible siamese mamandi brothers, the Barunbarun, live in a large cavern on the plateau, say the people of Oenpelli on the other side of the other end of the world without end; in the dreamtime they would sit all day long manufacturing stone spearheads. It is from them that our medicine-men acquired that art, which they subsequently passed on to us. Whosoever went near them would be speared. As for the Matjiba they live with their wives and families among the rocks, and if they see a lone traveller they catch him with a hooked stick around his neck or in his hair, then kill him. They heat a number of stones in a fire, lay their victim flat out on the ground, place the burning-hot stones on him, cover him with paper-bark, then with earth, and leave the body in this oven for a long time because they like their meat well cooked. When they think the meat is sufficiently tender they remove it from the oven, wrap it in clean paper-bark and carry it to their families in their dwelling-places red nudge, nudge, wink, wink, say no more, it's free massage week at 14 Howard Rd Beverley; AAA for any type of massage by new girls call at 149 Findon Rd; kisses AAA are you looking for the mature, experienced girl? For a massage at your place red I've brought with me a little sheet of paper with the following outline: The Spirit of the Place three, Boomerang: The Ceremony I Missed; Bicentenary Kit, Braisîle (carnival and processions), Australia (Brisbane diary), Japan (transistors and monasteries), Jungle (animals from Buffon), plus Nice and Geneva. In the plane, on my walks, I turn it all over in my mind, Marie-Jo darling, and I'd like to tell you how all this magma is developing. The Ceremony I Missed should be the account of my trip to Vancouver Island to see the potlatch that in the end didn't take place, while you were going to Zuni to see the Shalako. As for Brazil, I want to make a kind of fantastic carnival alternating continuously between Rio and Nice. The part on Japan will probably be called Archipelago

LYRE-BIRD   (O O)   TASMANIA   (O O)   SILVER   (O O)   GREVILLEA will consist of short pieces which move around as if in those inscriptions *small ads* (0 0) LETTERS FROM THE ANTIPODES (0 0) red carnival dream I meet a lady aged 50, young looking and young at heart, tired of being alone, who informs me that she wishes to meet a gentleman of similar age with a view to marriage, but makes clear that only genuine people should apply. She assures me that a sincere enquirer will not be disappointed. I am 29, high up in a bank and earn 4,200F a month; I have an apartment with a garden, a red car, am generous, sensitive, even sentimental, and wish to marry a woman between 23 and 30, sincere, affectionate, feminine, not superficial. I speak about this to a friend who is a tradesman of 27 earning 3,100F a month in a stable job, affectionate, sentimental, also with a red car, who loves music and animals and wishes to marry a woman between 19 and 27, gentle, quiet, not necessarily beautiful, but sensible, catholic. We explain our problems to a very handsome person of 50, 178 cm, professional man, well off, elegant, traditional type education but not snobbish, who confides in us that for him, it's a woman between 38 and 48 he wishes to marry, supportive, interested in sport, sea, sun, travel. At that very moment a secretary aged 37 comes by, who tells us of her optimism and zest for life, her femininity, earns 3,000F a month, owns an apartment and a red car, 158 cm, good figure, long hair, who tells whoever listens that she wishes to bring happiness to a man of distinction and charm between 45 and 50. We leave them together. Will something happen? Will he succeed in bridging the abyss of the year's age difference? And we continue our search in the public rooms of the big hotel to which we have been admitted to spend the night *red carnival dream* (0 0) LETTERS FROM THE ANTIPODES (0 0) *health problems* The infant mortality rate of Aborigines, already one of the highest in the world, has increased dramatically in the Alice Springs area this year. Our special correspondent Cameron Forbes has been investigating the tragedy. Tiny Mary lies still in her cot, a tube taped to her nose, her hands bound to keep it there

CENTAUR   (0 0)   KANGAROO   (0 0)   NORTHERN TERRITORY   (0 0)   PEARL

Mary is not very ill. She is in hospital because she has gastro-enteritis, because she is weak and exhausted after battling for most of her short life to stay alive. And if she is in this hospital, with its lack of staff and facilities, it is because she is an Aborigine red the piece on Australia will be called Letters from the Antipodes, Marie-Jo darling; it will consist of part of these letters and a certain number of other elements that will become clearer during my stay. Kisses. There is of course a very American side to present-day Australia, but what I am interested in is precisely the difference, and I will have to find new solutions. The jungle is there to link the other elements by reference to Black Africa or other equatorial regions which I don't know at first hand. I want to create a kind of forest of phrases traversed by animals by using Buffon's descriptions published shortly before the earliest serious knowledge of Australia became available. So I went to see if there was a Buffon in the University library, and I found it, but not with the French authors; it's in another building with the biology collection red Brampton Island, what are you thinking about Irène, what are you looking at, every day's a lazy day on Brampton Island at the other end of the world, enjoy it, from seawater pool to barbeque and bar. After dark there are parties, films, organized games. Relaxing comes easy at Brampton Island red the terrible mamandi Marliili, his daughter Mali and her fiancé Moia live in a large paper-bark hut in the jungle near the river where Moia spends his days hunting and fishing, say the people of Oenpelli on the other side of the other end of the world; they are all invisible and should anyone go near, Marliili follows his tracks and causes him to fall sick by pointing a bone at him which projects from his elbow. If ever we were to walk through their camp, we would be immediately transfixed by an invisible lance leaving an invisible fatal wound red AAA for a new and exciting massage, two girl massage

VERTICORDIA   (0 0)   CHAMELEON   (0 0)   EMU   (0 0)   VICTORIA

AAAt your service, 56 Grange Rd, Welland, open for massage from 10 in the morning until midnight from Monday to Saturday, Patricia, Maria and Nick, on the other side of the other end of the world without end; AAA sweethearts, beautiful clean young girls to massage you at your choice, hotel, motel, home: AAAristocratic, very cheap massage: French $A10, model $A10, extra special $A10 red in the subject catalogue: Camden Park, Australia's oldest pastoral property, far away; Herbert Evatt: Rum Rebellion, a study of the overthrow of Governor Bligh by John MacArthur and the NSW Corps; M. Jennings: John MacArthur and the Golden Fleece red what are the main features of the Aborigine's world? The natural world: provides food and raw materials, far, far away. Economic life: the Aborigines are semi-nomadic hunters, fishermen and collectors of food. Technology: they exploit the environment with implements, arms, boats and other objects. Social organization: classifies individuals and codifies behaviour in a tribe by their kinship, age, marriage, clan and local grouping. Tribes are usually divided into two moieties and four or eight sections. Members of a clan, moiety or section cannot intermarry. Religion links the Aborigines and nature through ancestral beings, the pre-existence and reincarnation of spirits, totemism, mythology, ritual and sanctions in the next world. Aesthetic expression: a rich heritage of art and a wealth of song, dance and oral literature red it can be seen that out of these 13 voyages round the world, not one originated in France at the end of the world, and that six only were made in the name of discovery BOUGAINVILLE that is those of Magellan, Drake, Lemaire, Roggeveen, Byron and Wallis: the other navigators whose sole aim was to enrich themselves by privateering against the Spanish, followed known routes without extending knowledge of the globe red when one of us dies, he is embalmed in several layers of paper-bark, say the people of Yirrkala at the other end of the world, and tied up with grass-string

CORAL   (O O)   NUYTSIA   (O O)   COMPASSES   (O O)   OPOSSUM meanwhile others are erecting a platform of branches and covering it with a layer of leaves red the people of Fingal TAS tell how a young settler built a house to live in with his bride who was still in England. He was so anxious to see her that he sailed without having finished his dwelling on the other side of the other end of the world. On learning that he had been jilted, he returned to Tasmania and hanged himself in the courtyard of his unfinished home which has been abandoned ever since. He haunts it, but no longer alone, accompanied as he is by a woman and child who rashly came to fetch water from his well and were drowned in it red China had been trading with the western Pacific islands for a thousand years before the Europeans arrived at the beginning of the 16th century. Once Portugal had gained control of the Indian Ocean route to the East Indies, on the other side of the other hidden end of the faraway world without end, the Spanish began to think of sailing there from America. In 1520–21 Ferdinand Magellan (portrait further round the map on the wall of my room in college) was the first European to do so. The Spanish captains who followed him included Alvaro de Mendaña and his lieutenant Pedro Fernandez de Quiros (portraits) who dreamt of a great southern continent red a quite high point of land to the NNW, far away, I named it Cape Byron COOK it can be recognized by a remarkably pointed mountain lying inland at NW by W red but it was the women in particular who aroused the pity of the female travellers. Nothing can compare with the condition of the Australian female; far, far away; cruel nature has denied her even the smallest degree of charm VERNE she's a slave, carried off by brute force, with no wedding present save blows from a waddie, a kind of stick permanently attached to her master's hand. From this moment on, the victim of premature and devastating old age, she is overwhelmed by all the arduous tasks of a nomadic life, carrying her children swathed in reeds together with fishing and hunting implements, supplies of "phormium tenax" with which she makes nets

RUBY   (0 0)   CALYTHRIX   (0 0)   DOVE   (0 0)   ECHIDNA she must find provisions for her family; she hunts lizards, opossums and snakes right up into the treetops; she chops firewood; she strips off bark for the tent; a poor beast of burden, she knows no rest, and it is only when her master has finished that she can eat his revolting leftovers red back home at The Antipodes I'm going through the things I brought back from my second trip to Australia: two watercolour landscapes done by Aborigines at Hermannsburg, kisses, an abstract gouache painting from Ernabella mission, five gouache paintings done by aboriginal children aged from 10 to 12 at the Hermannsburg school on the theme: Australia, four pastels by children from six to eight at the same school on the theme of an outing; reproduction of a series of 12 coloured late 19th century lithographs, sketches of Australian life and landscapes red the whale on the back of a bark painting: three Aboriginal fishermen went out in a canoe to catch turtles. They speared an enormous one, but as they couldn't manage to pull it out, one of them dived in. At that moment two large whales surfaced, swamping the boat. The diver tried to climb up by the prow, but swam right into the mouth of one of the monsters. His companions saw his legs struggling outside. His body was discovered on the beach the next day. The whale's wake is shown, and the light patches on his back characteristic of his species *labels* (0 0) LETTERS FROM THE ANTIPODES (0 0) *the bunyip* long before the White Man, the Aborigines believed in the existence of a monstrous dark creature that lived in the swamps, lagoons and billabongs of their tribal lands red fishing expedition on the back of a bark painting: as the turtle and the canoe with men did not take up fully the available space, the artist has introduced two dugongs; the turtle which has been speared by the fisherman seated in the prow is held by a fibre rope attached to the spearhead. Kisses. The canoe is down by the bow; the remaining two men try to trim it with their oars red Kilna has several hundred blacks—men, women and children—who live in shapeless bark huts (in Mistress Branican). What are you reading Mathilde? These Aborigines

SOUTH   (0 0)   SAPPHIRE   (0 0)   MACROZAMIA   (0 0)   SOUTHERN CROWN some of whom are remarkable specimens, tall, with statuesque proportions, robust and lithe, endowed with a tireless constitution, are well worth observing. Far away. They are mostly characterized by the typically shallow facial angle found in savage races VERNE they have prominent eyebrows, wavy or frizzly hair, a narrow forehead that recedes beneath their hair, a flat nose with broad nostrils, an enormous mouth with powerful teeth like those of a wild animal red back home at The Antipodes I'm still going through the objects brought back from my second trip to Australia: two plates from the Australian Resource Atlas 1) surface water 2) rainfall; two copies of the sightseeing map of central Australia 1) with a hand-drawn map in three colours on the back, done by a travel agent, setting out the Alice Springs-Hermannsburg route with detours to Standley Chasm, Glen Helen Gorge and Palm Valley, with a more detailed map of Hermannsburg and one of Standley Chasm 2) with a map in red biro on the front showing the route to Ayers Rock and the Olgas, with thick red marks made by dusty fingers; far, far away; a pale blue case bought at Alice Springs red full-length portrait: white dress with gold buttons, buckled shoes, royal blue coat, telescope in the right hand, scroll in the other, on the wall of my room in college, the hero of British eighteenth century ventures in the Pacific (including the voyages of Wallis and Carteret whose journals he consulted), James Cook destroyed the myth of the Great Southern Continent by mapping the East coast of Australia, circumnavigating New Zealand at the end of the world and going south as far as the polar circle, was killed by the Hawaiians on his third voyage (blue and white lying on the ground, redcoats taking aim, the natives naked apart from their chief wearing a superb headdress and coat of yellow and red feathers) after his vain search for the famous NW passage red at daybreak we were surprised to find that we were further South than the previous day

DRAGON LIZARD   (0 0)   WESTERN   (0 0)   GOLD   (0 0)   MELALEUCA and yet a strong Southerly had blown all night. We could make out the breakers at the other end of the hidden world. This is always likely to happen in the vicinity of the pointed mountain to the SE which I have already mentioned, and which for this reason I have named Mount Warning COOK is seven or eight leagues inland at 28°22′S. The surrounding country is elevated and uneven, but it is sufficiently noticeable to form a landmark red when one of us dies, we sing a new series of hymns and lays belonging to his group, say the people of Yirrkala on the other side of the other end of the world, and two of us mount the platform and dispose the body so that it faces the sky red the people of Munro QLD tell how the Englishman Dick Grover on the other side of the other end of the world without end fell into a sack containing 200 pounds of flour and died of suffocation; his white ghost haunts the plain red how do Aboriginal women live? They gather food, especially plants, in forests, marshes, lakes and along river banks, far away, fish, shellfish, crabs and other seafood among the rocky reefs; dig out yams and other roots with a sharpened stick, collect seeds and fruit, turtle and birds' eggs, catch lizards, snakes and other small animals; feed their family and friends, do most of the work around the camp, fetch drinking-water, firewood, look after the children and help put up the hut or shelter; weave sacks out of twine, baskets, mats and ornaments out of plant-fibres and animal fur red in 1714 a Frenchman named La Barbinais Le Gentil set out as a passenger to trade along the coasts of Chile and Peru. He then travelled to China, and after spending nearly a year there in different trading-posts, far, far away, he took a different boat from the one that had brought him and returned to Europe BOUGAINVILLE so that he had really travelled round the world himself, although it could not be considered a circumnavigation mounted by the French nation red AAA next week will be bearable after a massage at Carole's at the hidden end of the faraway world

CROW   (O O)   PLATYPUS   (O O)   NEW SOUTH WALES   (O O)   PLATINUM

AAA Maxine's, a luxurious massage in your hotel, motel or home, beautiful girls, couples a speciality, masseur available, 24 hour service; AAA reminder, Lady Godiva has moved to 206A Hutt Street, City, where she hopes to see her regular customers red on the back of the $A2 note ears of corn and a bearded man with rimmed glasses, chequered tie and white collar: Farrer. Nothing in the EB on him. DAB: William (1845–1906), wheat-breeder, born near Kendal, Westmorland, England at the other end of the world, 3 April. Began medical studies, but ill-health forced him to seek a warmer climate and he emigrated to Australia in 1870. Thought he would settle in the outback and took a post as a tutor with the family of George Campbell at Duntroon Station near Queanbeyan so that he could have time to find out about the area. The loss of his fortune made him give up the idea of buying land and in July 1875 he took his surveyor's examination, immediately found a job with the Department of Lands, and for the next 11 years, apart from a visit to England in 1878–9, he worked as a surveyor in NSW. Resigned in July '86 and withdrew to Lambrigg near Queanbeyan. Published in 1873: Grass and Sheep Farming, A Paper Speculative and Suggestive red food, glorious food at Brampton Island on the other side of the other end of the world, and plenty of it, all your meals served in the island's air-conditioned restaurant, with a magnificent selection of wines. If you've landed a fish during the day, our chef will cook it for you. Tea and coffee are served after meals in the recreation hall, and if you still feel the need for a bite, the snack bar is open from ten in the morning to three in the afternoon and again from nine to 11 in the evening red the terrible Waramuntjuna spirits live on turtles, say the people of Oenpelli on the other side of the other hidden end of the vast world without end and get cross when we capture a big one, since they regard them as their property.

LESCHENAULTIA   (o o)   CUP   (o o)   LYRE-BIRD   (o o)   QUEENSLAND with a flick of a finger they send a huge wave to swamp our boat, then take the turtle and bring it back to life by breathing on it. They put feathers in their hair, walk with a limp and play the drone tube red it is estimated that in 1971 infantile mortality will exceed the '70 figure of 182 per 1,000, at least five times that of white children. Kisses. If she were white, Mary would certainly not have suffered arrested growth, nor would she have spent 13 of the last 15 weeks in hospital and the two remaining ones on a dusty station, surrounded by dogs, filth and flies. If she is at risk in the camp, she is still at risk in Alice Springs Hospital. A number of babies, officially seven, who had just got over gastro-enteritis, caught measles and died red I went to the biological sciences library, Marie-Jo darling, and found the Buffon there, it's an old edition dated 1818 and I believe I'm the first person to borrow it since it was acquired. I intend to include in each section a little dream that will lead into one of the other countries that are treated; it would even be possible to include four dreams in each region, one for each of the others *health problems* (0 0) LETTERS FROM THE ANTIPODES (0 0) *vocabulary* Aussie = Australian; Tassie = Tasmanian red as for Australia, Marie-Jo darling, these are the main themes I want to treat: distance (this letter-diary will do, kisses, but I would also have liked to show how the press presents France, what gets through this far away—for instance, by studying a newspaper for a month, cutting out all the references to our country; it's much more difficult than it appears: you'd have to read nearly all the paper very carefully; students would have to do it for me; I don't know if I'll manage it), and the distances within the country

DIAMOND   (0 0)   BORONIA   (0 0)   SOUTHERN CROSS   (0 0)   KANGAROO its recent rather than modern character (when you go to the United States, even today, it's as if you're taking a journey into your future, but when you come to Australia, it's as if you're travelling in the past of the United States), the strangeness of the Australian bush, of course, with the obsession of death in the red desert, the Aborigines who are like subterranean Indians, kept much further away, even lower down the scale, and the reversals (the fact that winter is our summer, that the Sun is in the North at midday, etc.) red the descriptions of the bunyip given by the Aborigines vary enormously, Cécile, what are you thinking about, but they are all agreed on its sinister shining eyes on the other side of the other hidden end of the vast world, its bellowing red the terrible Nadubi spirits live in the scrub surrounding the springs at the base of the plateau, say the people of Oenpelli on the other side of the other end of the world without end, steal our meat, our honey and our best embers as they growl in the dark. They have barbed spikes coming out of their knees, their elbows and their sex organs, and they spear us with them if they find us drinking at springs on our own, and our medicine men can usually do nothing for us red at this time there were often two babies to a cot in the Alice Springs hospital, a nurse claimed there had been as many as three, with some in cardboard boxes on the floor. Far away. She looks around, remembering with horror how babies would be found dead in their cots for no apparent reason red on the front of the purple, pink and yellowish-green $A5 note, next to some specimens of eucalypts and banksias, the portrait of Banks; EB: Sir Joseph (1743–1820), English explorer and naturalist far, far away, better known for his patronage and encouragement of other scientists than for his own work. Born London, 2 February, educated at Harrow, Eton and Oxford, inherited his father's substantial fortune, voyages to Newfoundland and Labrador (1766), around the world with James Cook ('68–'71), to Iceland ('72), became president of the Royal Society in '78

TASMANIA   (0 0)   OPAL   (0 0)   ISOPOGON   (0 0)   SWORDFISH at his own expense or in his capacity of honorary director of the Royal Botanic Gardens at Kew, he sent out many collectors to various parts of the world. His house was for many years a place for naturalists to meet and have discussions red the main problem on Brampton Island is deciding what to do first. Take your time at the end of the world, you'll make up your mind while you're tanning on the beach, diving into the big, circular seawater pool, or lazing at the bar. You can play golf on the six hole course (watch out for the emu that loves stray balls!), there's always a game of tennis or table-tennis on, or darts and quoits, all tempting you to come to Brampton Island red let us now speak of those who, setting out either from Europe, or from the west coast of South America, or from the East Indies, have made discoveries in the South Seas at the other hidden end of the vast world without having gone round it BOUGAIN-VILLE it appears that it was a Frenchman, Paulmier de Gonneville, who made the first of these in 1503 and '04; it is not known where the places lie at which he landed and whence he brought back an inhabitant whom the government did not send back to his own country, but whom Gonneville, feeling a sense of personal responsibility towards him, married off to his heiress red AAA Main North Road Clinic, for the most relaxing massage of any type. Come and see Sue or Rose, parking at rear; AAA Bushman's Casino, quality massage, new girls, $A20 maximum for our specials; AAA the Pink Panther, new French specialties, come quick and see Sharon and Penny red the people of Guyra NSW tell how a workman's house was disturbed for months. Showers of stones came through the windows, and the entire building was shaken as if by giant hands. The police failed to find anything. About this time Mrs Doran disappeared without trace at the age of 87 red how to the Aboriginal men live? They are hunters and fishermen and kill kangaroos

EMU   (0 0)   NORTHERN TERRITORY   (0 0)   CARBUNCLE   (0 0)   CROTALARIA opossums, emus and other large game with spears or clubs, far away, or capture them in pit-falls, nets, traps or noose snares, smoke wombats and other mammals out of their burrows, throw their boomerangs among flocks of birds, spear fish or catch them with their bare hands, with nets, traps or hooks, or poison pools with certain plant juices (in the North they harpoon turtles, dugongs, porpoises and large fish), make weapons, implements, canoes, containers and ceremonial objects, the elders form a council responsible for the maintenance of law and custom; they are a stone-age people with their stone knives, scrapers, adzes, borers, axes, files, grinders, and also use wood, shell, bones and teeth red from Cape Moreton the land extended Westwards as far as we could see, far, far away, some on board thought there was a river there, because the sea was paler than usual COOK it was a point that could not be cleared up as we had the wind with us, but should anyone wish to do so he can always make out three hills to the North at 26°53'S. They lie a little inland and are not far from one another, easily recognizable by their outline which makes them look like glasshouses, which name I gave them red when one of us dies, say the people of Yirrkala at the hidden end of the vast world, once he is placed on the platform, we blow in a drone tube in order to warn the angels of the dead to come and occupy him so that he is prevented from tormenting his relatives. At the same time one of us climbs a tall tree to make the call of the nocturnal karawak bird, the messenger of the angels, and as soon as he hears them cough, he hastens down and flees with the rest of us, for the spirits and souls of the dead are dangerous to the living red back home at The Antipodes 12 seashells sent from Brisbane red the Dutch East India Company had dominated Pacific trade and exploration during the 17th century. One of its employees, Abel Tasman (portrait further round the map on the wall of my room in college), during his voyage in 1642–3 (Dutch galleon sailing in towards Hobart), was the first European to sight Tasmania

ERIDANUS   (0 0)   OPOSSUM   (0 0)   VICTORIA   (0 0)   ELIXIR on the other side of the other end of the world New Zealand and Fiji red the morning star on the back of a bark painting: two women have imprisoned the star all day and all evening in a bag represented by the swelling at the base of the stem in the middle. The painting is also said to represent a yam and its tuber. The knurls on the upper branches are the fruits, kisses, and their ends carry blossom. The knurls on the other branches represent places where creepers have twisted round. This remarkable painting is also a simplified map of Arnhem Land, with each blossom representing a village red these people of the NW are probably a mixed Australian and Papuan strain. Like others of the same origin, the Indas have long, curly hair VERNE they are lighter-skinned than the natives from the Southern provinces, who seem to constitute a more vigorous race; their proportions, which are more modest, give them an average height of 130 centimetres. The men are physically better constituted than the women; if their forehead is somewhat receding, it still stands out above their quite prominent brow ridges—which is a sign of intelligence, if we are to believe anthropologists; their eyes, with dark irises, have intense sparkling pupils *the equivocal racism of Uncle Jules* (0 0) LETTERS FROM THE ANTIPODES (0 0) *the natural stone* the opal is a form of hydrated silica. Its kaleidoscope of patterns, colours and degrees of transparency is caused by the refraction of white light passing through ultramicroscopic, regularly arranged spheres of various sizes. The smaller spheres produce the greens and violets, the larger, the yellows and reds red the Australian negro is endowed with an extraordinary sense of smell which is on a par with the best hunting dogs. He can pick up human or animal scent by merely sniffing the ground, and by smelling grass and scrub. Kisses. His auditory nerve is also extremely sensitive, and it appears that he can hear the sound of ants working in the depths of an anthill VERNE as for placing these natives among the ranks of climbers, this would not be unreasonable

REGELIA   (0 0)   FURNACE   (0 0)   ECHIDNA   (0 0)   PLASTIC for no gum tree is too high and smooth for them to reach its tip by using a flexible rattan rope to which they give the name "kâmin" and also thanks to the slightly prehensile nature of their toe red European deserters in the Pacific had already been forced to show that it was possible to cover long distances in small, open boats, as the Polynesians had done. What are you dreaming about, Agnès, what are you reading? One of the most detailed accounts of such a journey is by Captain Bligh (portrait further round the map on the wall of my room in college) who, after a mutiny on his ship the Bounty in 1789, sailed 3,600 miles to Timor in its longboat (illustration showing them setting out) with 18 of her crew at the other end of the world. Nine of the mutineers, taking several Tahitian men and women with them, sailed on to the deserted island of Pitcairn where some of their descendants still live red spearing, cutting up and cooking a turtle on the back of a bark painting: at the top two men from Yirrkala in a boat have speared the turtle; at the bottom they are sitting round a fire on which the animal is cooking on the other side of the other end of the world. It has been cut into pieces. The large oval represents its shell red when one of us dies, say the people of Yirrkala on the other side of the other hidden end of the dazzling world without end, for two or three months nobody goes near the burial platform. When the maggots that fed on his body have entered the ground and turned into flies, we come and cleanse his bones. We dance and sing at length to the accompaniment of music sticks and drone tubes, and this keeps the spirits away. The skeleton is brought down, laid on the ground between two seated men, while a third thrusts a spear between its ribs, saying that he is spearing a turtle red back home at The Antipodes books brought or sent back from my second trip: Eucalypts, Australian Butterflies, far away, The Hidden Face of Australia red what are the Aborigines' dwelling-places like? Each family has its own hut and fire-place, far, far way, youths and single men occupy a separate part

BEAUFORTIA   (O O)   CRANE   (O O)   DRAGON LIZARD   (O O)   SOUTH the huts are round or rectangular. Their covering varies according to the region: branches, grass, bark, reeds, palm-leaves, seaweed; they are sometimes smeared with mud. Communal huts are built in cold weather or when there are too many mosquitoes. Food is baked in hot ashes or roasted. In many tribes the men cook large animals in pits lined with heated stones and covered with soil and bark. Meat is shared among all members of a camp according to family hierarchy. Nuts and seeds are preserved for several months in pits, fish and kangaroo-meat are dried, and a kind of cake called damper is made red pleasant Southerly breezes, at ten o'clock yesterday we passed at a distance of four miles and in 17 fathoms a sheer black rock (or peninsula) on which a number of natives were assembled at the end of the world, which occasioned my naming it Indian Head red AAA Cinderella's, hotel, motel, at home or studio, we're back again with new lovelies, everyone welcome from Prince Charming to Ugly Duckling, also an irresistible masseur, it's fun at Cinderella's at the other end of the world; AAA movie massage, Japanese or French massage, discreet, warm, friendly surroundings, fully carpeted, also Ian the versatile masseur, and don't forget Pinky red the people of Yallourn VIC tell how last century a herd of wild cattle stampeded through the hamlet of Moe in the Gippsland Hills. Some farmers set out to find the missing drover, and found the remains of his camp on the other side of the other hidden end of the dazzling world, but nothing else. Some time later another herd passing by the same spot panicked in a similar way. The drover stated that he had heard a ghost herd and the cracking of stockwhips. The next time a whole group of people accompanied the stock over the hills; they became restless at night, and two men were sent to see what was happening on the other side

STRAW　　(0 0)　　CALOTHAMNOS　　(0 0)　　CLOCK　　(0 0)　　PLATYPUS

came back pale with fear, having seen nothing but with their ears still ringing with the extraordinary noises that had pursued them. Ever since then no cattle have gone there red pick any of Brampton Island's scenic walks—the one to Turtle Bay is among the most delightful—and you can take along a free picnic or barbeque lunch. You can go oystering on the rocks, fish underwater or off the jetty in more leisurely fashion, or admire the coral from our glass-bottomed boat. Take a fun cruise, learn to water-ski or improve your style behind the ski boat on Brampton Island red after Gonneville and Magellan, far away, the Spaniard Alfonso de Salazar discovered in 1525 the Isle of Saint Bartholomew BOUGAINVILLE at 14°N and about 158°E of Paris red it is not in Alice Springs that the major problem lies, but out in the enormous expanse of the Centre, in the camps, stations, farms, missions where the Aborigines live. The fault does not lie with the little hospital or its overworked staff, but with white society. Far, far away. If we had a 300-bed hospital, it would be full tomorrow, a doctor stated. Ten per cent of Aboriginal children in the area are in hospital all the time until they are two red Sir Joseph Banks in the DAB: President of the Royal Society, known as the father of Australia, hardly distinguished himself at Eton although he showed an interest in botany and natural history in general, at the end of the world, once at Oxford showed just as little disposition to study except in his favourite subjects, kept up his interest in science after inheriting his father's large fortune and made friends among the scientists of his day, was elected to the Royal Society in '66, made a research trip to Newfoundland and Labrador in the same year, sailed with James Cook on the Endeavour in August '68 and was away nearly three years. The main object of the expedition was to observe the transit of Venus

WESTERN   (O O)   BARK   (O O)   WARATAH   (O O)   SEA SERPENT also sailed round the world landing in many countries including New Zealand and Australia, immediately became famous on his return to England, wished to accompany Cook again, but difficulties about accommodation for his assistants made him give up the idea red the bunyip has an enormous body covered with fur or feathers, and in place of its legs there are flippers that thrash the water when it is angry at the other hidden end of the dazzling world, it devours people, coming upon them in silence when least expected red the terrible mamandi Nabarakbia lives in caves whose entrances under banyan trees are no larger than those of a bandicoot burrow, say the people of Oenpelli on the other side, he mainly eats fish but loves stealing the spirits of sick people, which he cooks and eats. It is then too late for our medicine-men to do anything red Pommie = English; kisses; Frenchie = Frenchman red all of a sudden the light went out, Marie-Jo darling; it was just as the Sun was setting. A break in supply caused by the strike. As I had neither candles nor torch, there was nothing to do except go out. I wandered around campus to see if there were lights anywhere. All the buildings were dark, all the street lights were out. The birds began to call. It was like being in a total eclipse. Far off however, on the other side of the river, the bright lights of the city centre were on, and on the hills, the red lights of the television transmitters. In some of the buildings around me there were emergency lights working off standby generators. I wondered how I was going to manage to eat, but as I got back to college I saw the flicker of candles in the dining-room; dinner was being served, and I joined the handful of students; the light came back on at dessert time; the breakdown lasted half an hour; all the campus clocks are electric; they all started again half an hour late and most are still not showing the official time

LYRE-BIRD   (O O)   NEW SOUTH WALES   (O O)   PAPER   (O O)   ANIGOSANTHOS

then I was taken to the wine and cheese party *vocabulary* (o o) LETTERS FROM
THE ANTIPODES (o o) *the red and black day* distributed by OPAL (One People
of Australia Limited): conscious of the fact that to date Australian history books
have paid little attention to the presence of Black Australians, the Committee
for the Observance of National Aborigines' Day (14 July) has asked a Black
Australian to write the missing chapter: the Aborigines have lived in Australia
since time immemorial red at last I've found some very fine boots, Marie-Jo
darling, not without difficulty, kisses, Australian ones in the largest shop, Myer
(the biggest chain-store organization in the whole of Australia with its head
office in Melbourne), but unfortunately they didn't have my size; the salesman
kindly telephoned their Indooroopilly branch where they had it. I found the
Aboriginal Affairs office and its shop; they've got some nice things. Then lunch
with someone from the department of fine arts, an appointment at two o'clock
with some people in the department of music. My programme is becoming more
and more precise, and in the end I'm going to have a lot to do (so much the
better!), but it'll be nearly all over by the time you arrive, because on 15 August
there's another vacation period that lasts until the end of our stay red opal
was first mined commercially in 1875 at the township of Listowel Downs QLD.
What can you hear, Irène, where are you at the other end of the world? Previously it had been merely an object of curiosity without commercial value red
the terrible mamandi Adungun travelled all over the country in the dreamtime,
say the people of Oenpelli on the other side, feeding on our ancestors and vomit-
ing up their corpses; one day we managed to inflict so many spear wounds
on him that his stomach dropped out and he died red Blackie = Aborigine

HYDRUS   (o o)   KANGAROO   (o o)   QUEENSLAND   (o o)   WOOD mixie = mixed blood red His Majesty's Spanish Flock in the subject catalogue, Sir Joseph Banks and the Merinos of George III, far away; the Ceremony of the Unveiling of the Sir Joseph Banks Memorial by His Excellency Rt. Hon. W. J. McKell, Governor-general of the Commonwealth of Australia at Captain Cook's Landing Place red the Blacks always maintain that the bunyip prefers female flesh red after Alfonso de Salazar and Magellan, Alvaro de Saavedra set out from a Mexican port in 1526 at the end of the world, discovered a whole mass of islands BOUGAINVILLE between the ninth and 11th parallels North which he named the King's Isles, more or less at the same longitude as the Isle Saint Bartholomew; he then sailed on to the Philippines and the Spice Islands; and on his way back to Mexico, he was the first to discover the islands or lands named New Guinea and Papua. He further discovered at 12°N, about 80 leagues East of the King's Isles, a series of low-lying islands named the Bearded Isles red children come into hospital suffering from malnutrition. They are treated for as long as possible, at the risk of cross-infection, to build them up sufficiently before they are sent back out into the vast expanse of the Centre at the other end of the world. Like Mary, many will return red the people of Drysdale VIC tell how Miss Drysdale, the sister of an Edinburgh paymaster, arrived in the district at a fairly advanced age, on the other side of the other end of the world, and had a nice house called Coriyule with windows adorned with heraldic blazons built on the Bellarine peninsula. Three years after it was finished, she died and was buried along with her favourite horse on a nearby hilltop. The next owner had her coffin taken to the public cemetery. Ever since a ghostly piano accompanied by a mocking neighing has been heard red every morning at eight o'clock you'll find the day's activities pinned on the foyer notice board on Brampton Island

CEPHALOTUS   (0 0)   INDIAN   (0 0)   EMU   (0 0)   TASMANIA

you can do as much or as little as you like, either way you can count on having
the time of your life, far away, and the Dolphin and Mischief can be chartered
any time as well as a fibreglass catamaran on Brampton Island red gentle SSE
to SE breeze and fine weather, yesterday evening we steered through a passage
from three to six or seven miles wide and from eight to nine in length between
the continent to the West and the islands COOK the whole passage is one harbour with little bays and coves on each side where ships might lie as if in dock.
I named it Whitsunday Passage as we discovered it on that day, and the islands
I named Cumberland Isles in honour of the duke red AAA the Red Garter,
it's the talk of the town, exotic massages and girls, ask for Xavier; AAA hygienic
suburban parlour, suburban prices, all kinds of massage, including sauna at the
end of the world; at the Velvet Glove you can experience the most exciting
massage in Adelaide, even our low prices will excite you, correct English massage
a specialty, just let our girls get their hands on you red back home at The
Antipodes The Art of the Wandjina, A Line on Newcastle at the other end
of the world, Aboriginal Place Names, Paintings, Wild Life of Australia red
what is the Aborigines' economic life like? Collecting mussels, the hunter's spoils:
koala, wallaby, echidna, lizard and snake; the hunter quenches his thirst; making
a spear-thrower; a bark canoe; the women are skilled basket-makers; making
a bark container; baby minding red the Southern Cross on the back of a bark
painting: the four stars and the two of the compass are shown in the upper
part as a sting-ray being chased by a shark on the other hidden side of the
other end of the red world without end red when one of us dies, say the people
of Yirrkala far away, and the skeleton has been taken down from the platform,
the women who had been sitting at the side take it apart, wash the bones in
water and wrap them in paper-bark red for the Australian negroes life revolves
round a single act. "Ammeri! Ammeri!" this word recurs constantly

BRICK   (O O)   BUNYA   (O O)   HARE   (O O)   OPOSSUM in the Aboriginal tongue, kisses, and it means hunger VERNE the most frequent gesture of these savages consists in smacking their stomach, for their stomach is all too often empty. In these regions without game or crops, one eats at any time of day or night, whenever the opportunity arises, with the constant perspective of an impending and prolonged bout of fasting red Micronesia, small islands, on the wall of my room in college: people from Asia probably arrived there about 4,500 years ago, some who moved south and settled on Fiji and Tonga may have been the ancestors of the Polynesians, others may have settled on one of the many islands, for example, the high, volcanic Marianas, or coral islands such as the 1,156 atolls and reefs of the Marshall Islands. The inhabitants of this archipelago depend almost entirely on fishing, whereas the high islanders were able to grow a wide variety of crops. Inter-island trade has always played an important part in the life of the Micronesians who developed into remarkable navigators. Yap islanders used to sail as far as Palau to quarry the large discs of stone they still use as money (illustration). Ruins in the Caroline Islands, in particular those of Nan Matol on Ponape (illustration) show that the inhabitants were skilled builders before the Europeans arrived. Micronesian navigators used charts made of knurled sticks representing currents, studded with shells representing islands. Decorative panel at Palau *Australia unlimited* (0 0) LETTERS FROM THE ANTIPODES (0 0) *telephone* by dialling a number in Sydney you can hear Biblical gems accompanied by a tune red Polynesia, many islands, kisses, further round the map: excavations suggest that the ancestors of the Polynesians were making a living from fishing and agriculture on the South China coast 6,000 years ago. When the Chinese civilization to the North began to expand, some of these coast people may have sought new land in the Pacific

NORTHERN TERRITORY   (0 0)   STONE   (0 0)   BLACKBOY   (0 0)   WOLF

61

they may have moved slowly through Micronesia, arriving in Fiji about 1,500 BC, and entering the Polynesian triangle three centuries later. Carbon 14 dating suggests that by 500 AD they had already reached Easter Island. They .may have had contact with the west coast of America red when one of us dies, what are you thinking about, Mathilde, what are you up to, say the people of Yirrkala, other world, three days after they have washed the bones our women unwrap them, rub them with red ochre and place them in a temporary bark coffin on the outside of which his totemic symbol has been painted red what do these natives feed on—without doubt the most wretched of all the people whom nature has scattered over the surface of the continents? On a sort of rough cake called "damper", made from a little unleavened wheat, cooked not in an oven but under burning cinders—on honey that is sometimes gathered, far away, but only by felling the tree at the top of which the bees have made their hive—on "kedgeree", a kind of white gruel VERNE obtained by crushing the fruit of a poisonous palm tree whose toxins have been extracted by a series of delicate operations—on jungle hen's eggs, buried in the ground and artificially hatched by its heat—on the pigeons found only in Australia that hang their nests from the ends of tree branches. Finally they still use certain kinds of beetle larvae, some of which are gathered from acacia foliage, others being extracted from the mass of rotting wood littering the floor of the jungle ... And that's all red how do the Aborigines make fire? By friction or percussion. Far, far away. By simple rotation: a hollow is made in a softwood stick or a shield or log; the operator twirls a hardwood stick at a rapid rate between the palms of his hands as he moves them up and down it. The glowing powder is tipped onto tinder which is blown on gently and then swung in the air; it ignites after about a minute. The fire-saw: the edge of a hardwood stick is rubbed rapidly against a cleft stick with tinder in the cleft

ECHIDNA   (0 0)   VICTORIA   (0 0)   COPPER   (0 0)   EUCALYPTUS percussion: in SA a flint is struck with a piece of very hard stone, iron pyrites for example. The sparks ignite a tinder bed formed of dried grass, finely shredded bark, dead leaves, bird feathers or animal hair red dogs of Bahloo on the back of a bark painting: Bahloo the Moon had three snakes which were delightful and playful with him, but terrifying for the Aborigines. He called them his dogs at the end of the world. One night he descended to Earth and asked some Aborigines to take his dogs across a stream; they ran away in fright. As a punishment they have to remain dead once they are dead and cannot have monthly rebirth like the Moon. The Aborigines kill all the snakes they can find, but there will always be snakes because the Moon replaces them. It is portrayed here as a Wandjina, with his three snakes separated from the group of startled Aborigines by a stream red AAA open! open!! open!!! the Tigresses, special opening, with a team of specially selected young ladies who will revitalize you in an atmosphere of total relaxation; it's great, it's different, it's the latest thing in Adelaide; hunters, if you want the absolute, come along and hunt our tigresses, they're dying to get their claws into you; come along if you want to enjoy a massage with colour TV and refreshments at the other end of the world. AAA at Napoleon's, Waterloo Road, have you met your Waterloo yet? No? Then come along and see us, we promise you won't lose the battle, all our pretty masseuses are here to give you an experience you won't easily forget, our new "bunny" massage starts this week, and then there's our very new "black and white show"—you won't be disappointed, special foam baths and saunas to season our menu, relax with a glass in the comfortable men's lounge while you choose your massage and your masseuse, our pretty girls are waiting to take you prisoner, so don't miss out! Julie and Sue are back red back home at The Antipodes I'm listening to five records sent to me after my second journey

TABLE MOUNTAIN   (O O)   DRAGON LIZARD   (O O)   SILVER   (O O)   WATTLE red just say, and the night's yours on the other side of the other end of the world without end at Brampton Island—fancy dress balls or games, cabaret night on Monday when the musicians land and have as much fun as you—let your hair down and dance and sing until you're breathless on Brampton Island red this bay which I named Cleveland Bay appears to extend for five or six miles in each direction. I named the east point Cape Cleveland and the west point Magnetic Cape or Island COOK as it was very much like an island and the compass needle began to spin as we came near red Dr Kirke, Chairman of the Institute for Aboriginal Development, has studied infantile mortality in the Centre, and writes in his recently published thesis that "an enormous number of children die from apparently curable, if not preventable diseases far, far away". The main problem is malnutrition—in this fat and lucky country they simply die of hunger red the people of Berrima NSW tell how on 22 October 1842 Lucretia Dunkley, the licensee of the Three Legs Hotel, was hanged in the prison which had been built three years previously at the end of the world, because she had killed a rich farmer and robbed him of 500 sovereigns. Her head was removed for scientific examination. For years her headless ghost haunted the old pine trees in front of the prison; in the end they were cut down, but since then she has haunted the ruins of the old pub red a Murray River Aborigine drew a bunyip in 1848 at the other end of the world, with the body of a hippopotamus and the head of a horse red after Alvaro de Saavedra, Diego Hurtado and Hernando de Grijalva, who had set out from Mexico in 1433 on the other side in order to explore the South Seas BOUGAIN-VILLE only discovered an island situated at 20°30′N and about 100°W of Paris. They named it Saint Thomas Island red Johnnie = Chinese other world; commie = communist red an Account of the Voyages undertaken by the order of His present Majesty for making Discoveries in the Southern Hemisphere

MICROSCOPE   (0 0)   PLATYPUS   (0 0)   SOUTH   (0 0)   PEARL

and successively performed by Commodore Byron, Captain Wallis, Captain Carteret and Captain Cook in the Dolphin, the Swallow and the Endeavour, drawn
up from the journals which were kept by several commanders, and from the
papers of Joseph Banks in the author and title catalogue; Captain Cook's
Florilegium; a selection of engravings from the drawings of plants collected by
Sir Joseph Banks and Daniel Solander on Captain Cook's first voyage to the
islands of the Pacific red it was not until 1890 when two hunters collected a
large number of opals at White Cliffs NSW that their commercial value began
to go up. An Adelaide merchant gave 140 pounds for them, a considerable
sum for the time red in the dreamtime the terrible mamandi Boubitboubit only
ate wild honey, say the people of Oenpelli at the end of the world; one day,
while he was out searching for food, he noticed a swarm of bees in the hollow
branch of a tree on the edge of the Gudjamandi waterhole, cut a hole in the
branch with his stone axe and took out all the honey he could, ate part of
it and put the rest down beside him. Seeing that the hive extended further into
the tree, he made another hole nearer the ground so that he could get more
out, but the tree belonged to the rainbow-serpent Ngaloit who, when he heard
the buzzing of the bees, became so furious that he went up into the sky and
produced such heavy rain that he drowned Boubitboubit and his family; they
now live at the bottom of the waterhole beneath two trees, one covered with
blossom, the other old and dry but covered with hives. The Boubitboubit family
gather the honey in palm baskets or sacks of special herbs which they hang
up. With the first rains of the wet season, the spirit of one of our medicine-men
leaves his sleeping body to go to Gudjamandi, armed with powerful chants to
protect himself from the honey mamandi and to appease the rainbow-serpent.
Under his spell, the two Boubitboubit guards allow him to go down to the bottom, take the sacks of honey from the old tree, come back up to the surface
and throw them one after the other towards our settlements which he names
each in turn

BANKSIA   (O O)   FLY   (O O)   LYRE-BIRD   (O O)   WESTERN the Boubitboubit then notice that their honey has been stolen, but the chant continues to protect the spirit of the medicine-man from their fury and it reenters his body; thus we have five different kinds of honey in abundance; the black which is only found in trees; the peppery sort found more or less everywhere, the clear Boubit honey used by the Whites; the darker Laubun honey, and finally cristal honey red the Tasmanians, you can read at the Opal Centre, who were completely exterminated at the beginning of the European invasion, were possibly in Australia even before the Australians. Like the people of New Guinea and the Torres Strait, kisses, they seem to have been part of a Negroid migration starting in Africa and spreading to Micronesia and Melanesia in the Western Pacific red while we were in the music department, Marie-Jo darling, the French department rang MS to tell him that an Aboriginal woman poet wanted to see me; she had already phoned several days previously, but had left no means of contacting her. As I had told the journalists at the airport that I was also interested in the Aborigines and she had read it in the paper, she wondered if I could be encouraged to meet some of her friends who wrote like her. She was a curious person with a ballpoint pen behind her ear beneath her thick long black hair, obviously of mixed blood, probably no more than a quarter-cast Aborigine, very apprehensive at first, but I think the interview went off all right; she left me some of her poems which were either typed or published in leaflet form by the "Catholic Aboriginal Society" (although they're not exactly "catholic"), and I hope I can go and see her and her friends in the outlying suburb where she lives, an island between Brisbane Bay and the Pacific *the red and black day* (o o) LETTERS FROM THE ANTIPODES (o o) *red jungle dream* I can make enormous leaps with ease, the sudden movement of my tail is sufficient to knock down a man

CORAL   (O O)   CLIANTHUS   (O O)   LEVEL   (O O)   KANGAROO the ease with which I can move the skin on my face, and especially my brow, which greatly improves my appearance or rather the expression of my fury, and then my ability to move my mane, which not only bristles, but also moves and shakes in all directions when I am red with anger. Aelian and Oppian have seen in me Ethiopia coloured black like the men there, coloured white in India and sometimes marked or striped with different colours, red, black, yellow, turquoise, white, rainbow *red jungle dream* (0 0) LETTERS FROM THE ANTIPODES (0 0) *aboriginal astronomy* the people of Groote Eylandt believe that a small group of stars in our Hydra constellation is an unmarried crab-man, that the Milky Way is a celestial river full of large fish and waterlilies to which the inhabitants of the sky come for their food, that the tribe of the stars is divided into two moieties like their own, that Venus the man and Jupiter the woman have two children who are stars in the sting of our Scorpio, friends of the SE wind that blows at its full strength when they appear on the horizon on late April evenings red I've finally managed to buy those boots, Marie-Jo darling, they suit me very well and I shall be able to take them to Adelaide tomorrow for our mountain walks at the weekend. Kisses. I had asked if they could be paid for by cheque, and they had said yes of course, but when I made the cheque out they wanted my driving licence, and I said I hadn't got it on me and showed my passport instead; this caused so much confusion that in the end it was easier to tear up the cheque and pay cash. Tomorrow afternoon I take the plane to Melbourne and Adelaide, the only capital that is not a former penal colony red by dialling a number in Sydney, what are you up to Cécile, what are you eating far, far away, you can hear the boating weather red the terrible mamandi Dalbudia is like a man, he lives with his wife and children in the deep gloom of the caves, say the people of Oenpelli at the end of the world; being an excellent hunter, he normally leaves us alone, but if ever we were to go into his lair, he would attack us with his club red at the time when European emigration began the Aborigines

NEW SOUTH WALES   (0 0)   RUBY   (0 0)   HAKEA   (0 0)   OCTANT had a social order and an ecological culture that were probably unique in the history of mankind, you can read at the Opal Centre at the other end of the world, the nature of the country where there were no animals for domestication, no plants to grow and almost no rivers along which permanent dwelling places could be established red on the back of the $A5 note, next to a mass of female faces in front of a quay, with to the right a large sailing ship on the waves on the other hidden side of the other end of the inverted world, the portrait of Caroline Chisholm. The EB has nothing on her, the DAB: 1808–77, philanthropist, daughter of William Jones, a well-to-do farmer of Wootton, Northamptonshire, as a child met at her father's a wounded soldier who explained to her that he had been maimed while defending her, at 22 married Captain Chisholm, a quiet studious man, who shared her progressive ideas, and who two years later was sent to Madras, where she was able to see the neglected state of the soldiers' children and in particular the girls, founded the "female school of industry for the daughters of European soldiers" at which they learnt reading and writing, the catechism, cooking, housekeeping and nursing and which was taken over by Her Majesty's government when the Chisholms left for Australia in 1838 red in 1900 several thousand prospectors tried their luck at finding opals at White Cliffs on the other side of the other end of the world without end, and most of the stones discovered were sent to Germany for cutting and polishing red Jean Gaëtan set out from Mexico in 1542 far away, and also set his route to the North of the Line BOUGAINVILLE where he discovered between the 20th and ninth parallels, at different latitudes, several islands including Rocca Partida, the Coral Isles, the Garden Isles, the Sailor Isles, the Island of Arezifa, and finally he landed in New Guinea or rather, according to his account, New Britain, but Dampier had not yet discovered the passage that bears his name red surfie = surfer; far, far away; swaggie = tramp from the Centre red the people of Collector NSW tell how Johnny Gilbert, a young Canadian belonging to Ben Hall's gang

EMU   (0 0)   QUEENSLAND   (0 0)   SAPPHIRE   (0 0)   GREVILLEA had borrowed a racehorse from a farmer at the end of the world, solemnly promising to bring it back. In the meantime the police shot him. One night the farm people heard a wild neighing in the stables, went outside and saw Johnny's ghost closing the ranch gate. The horse was in its box red another drawing of the bunyip, by a native of VIC in the 19th century at the other inverted end of the hidden world, gives it the head and neck of an emu red a low green wooded island in the offing at N35°E, at a distance of three or four leagues NE½E from Cape Grafton, and I marked it on the chart by the name of Green Island on the other side of the other end of the world. As we came round the cape, we saw in the sandy cove a small stream, but did not go there in the boat because it seemed to me that landing would be difficult. We can say little about the country formed of steep rocky hills COOK the shore between Cape Grafton and the northern point forms a large but not very deep bay which I named Trinity Bay after the day on which we discovered it, and the point itself Cape Tribulation, for it is here that all our troubles began red in ten days, on 3 October 1971, 45-year-old Toby Ginger, camel hunter, stock- man, shearer and handyman on the other side of the other end of the world without end, will set out on his most important journey ever red back home at The Antipodes: Alice Springs and Ayers Rock in colour; Wild Australia, far away; Colonial Painters 1788–1880; Mark Twain, Following the Equator red on Lindeman Island you can take off in any number of directions far, far away— soak up the Sun, swim, go waterskiing, oystering or walking through National Park forests. Show me the way to Lindeman Island red Dinewan the emu and Goomblegubbon the turkey on the back of a bark painting: mother turkey was jealous of the emus who, in the dreamtime, could fly and were the kings of the air

PEACOCK   (0 0)   OPOSSUM   (0 0)   TASMANIA   (0 0)   GOLD she succeeded in persuading mother emu to cut off her wings and those of her family at the inverted end of the hidden world, but when she gathered her wits mother emu got her revenge on mother turkey by inducing her to kill all but two of her children. This is why emus can no longer fly, and Australian turkeys can only lay two eggs. The painting shows the stumpy-winged emu and her tracks, the stone axe with which she cut off her wings, and her family watching from behind a bush red Bluebeard's 15 young girls, all massages; Caribbean, new girls, massage from $A4 to $A10, Spanish or model, free sauna; Eve is back, phone for a fantastic massage; Europa Massages, new girls, new management, new prices red one of the natives, seizing a red painted instrument, in Captain Grant's Children, of unusual shape, left his companions who were still motionless on the other side, and made his way between the trees and bushes towards the band of cockatoos VERNE he made no noise as he crawled, neither brushing a leaf nor disturbing a stone. He was a moving shadow red what kinds of games and music do the Aborigines have? Children imitate adult life on the other side of the other faraway end of the forgotten world without end. Boys practise assiduously with toy weapons and at following tracks, girls play at making camps, and all learn songs, dances, tales, the art of drawing in the sand and making figures with the hands or with string held between the fingers (there are more than 200 kinds of these known in Australia). Children are treated with great affection. Adults are fond of ball games and spinning tops. The men have dart- and boomerang-throwing competitions; many are contests between the two moieties of the clan. Primitive musical instruments; everywhere a stick beaten on the ground or a pair of sticks or boomerangs are used to beat out time for the dances. In the North a wooden tube up to three metres long, the didgeridoo, produces a droning note

VERTICORDIA   (O O)   PHOENIX   (O O)   ECHIDNA   (O O)   NORTHERN TERRITORY in the South leaves were blown into. Dances imitate animals, humans and spirits, and each tribe had hundreds of chants forming sacred cycles red the Polynesians used double-hulled canoes up to 30 metres long for their long journeys, outrigger canoes and rafts for shorter journeys. Kisses. Boat construction was one of their most respected arts along with sculpture and tattooing. Polynesia is the home of surfing, known to the Hawaiians for hundreds of years. The conch shell is no longer used to warn of battle, but only in peaceful ceremonies red when one of us dies, once the women have washed his bones, say the people of Yirrkala, his skull is painted with his totemic signs and placed in a reed basket which one of his close female relatives carries with the temporary bark coffin from camp to camp so that it may be mourned and his soul thus rendered happy *the groves of death* (0 0) LETTERS FROM THE ANTIPODES (0 0) *the asylum* although Western Australia is proud of the fact that it was originally settled by free Whites alone, in 1850, 21 years after its foundation, it succeeded in persuading the imperial government to send convict ships, although they had already ceased coming to the continent's other colonies. This lasted until 1868. One of their first tasks was the building of a lunatic asylum, now Fremantle Museum. The Eendracht gallery, named after Dirck Hartog's boat which landed in WA in 1616, introduces the theme of discovery. Near the entrance: replica of the warped pewter plate, today in the Amsterdam Rijksmuseum, which was left by Dirck Hartog and his sailors of the East India Company on the island near Shark Bay which bears his name. The post bearing it is the one left on the same spot by Willem de Vlamingh in 1797, who copied the original inscription onto another plate and added an inscription in his own hand. In other display cases the events leading up to the first European voyages to the Indian Ocean and eventually to Australia are related

PLATINUM   (0 0)   NUYTSIA   (0 0)   PAINTER   (0 0)   DRAGON LIZARD there is also a large cannon from the wreck of the Batavia red when one of us dies, his temporary bark coffin is hung on a pair of forked sticks, and the bag with his skull on the branch of a tree, say the people of Yirrkala, kisses, then after several months, when the old men decide that the time has come, the dead man's brothers cut down a hollow tree to make his wooden coffin, and after taking off its bark, paint his totemic signs on it red how do the Aborigines dress and adorn themselves? What are you doing Agnès, what are you dreaming about? Either they go completely naked on the other side of the other faraway end of the forgotten world, or they use a pubic apron of fur or string attached to a girdle. Everyday ornaments consist of a girdle, bracelets, necklet, forehead-band, and nose-pin. On festive occasions, they wear special clothes of many kinds together with designs painted on the body in red, yellow, white or black, and in feather-down stuck on with human blood. They scar themselves with knives made of shell or stone, and the wound is filled with ashes until it heals to form a thick weal. The designs may cover men from the shoulder to the knee. Some patterns belong to certain tribes, some are added at initiation, marriage, or some other important stage of life; the most complex of them thus form a purely individual work red cutting into the South of the map on the wall of my room in college to reach the two islands: New Zealand is a mountain range on the eastern edge of the land mass that includes Australia. Its volcanoes and earthquakes are, like those of Japan, typical of the reliefs that have emerged all around the Pacific, other world. Many volcanoes in the North Island are still active. There are also geysers and hot springs. The Southern Alps, a 480 km long fold forming the backbone of the South Island, culminate in Mount Cook (3,764 m). Maori legends tell how the navigator Kupe discovered the country a thousand years ago. Excavations seem to indicate that the first Polynesians did arrive from Tahiti at that time

VICTORIA   (0 0)   DIAMOND   (0 0)   CALYTHRIX   (0 0)   SOUTHERN FISH

archeologists call them moa-hunters, after the great wingless birds they exterminated red Hud is new and different, for the massage that will at last give
you satisfaction, see the masseur who knows, far away; Liz will give you an
experience that will send you out of your mind, a magic massage; for a stimulat-
ing massage come to the Casbah to see Koby and Kaby and our new girl
Leighanne red when he was at a suitable distance, the savage threw his
instrument in a horizontal direction two feet off the ground. The weapon in
question covered around 40 feet in this manner; then suddenly, without touching
the earth, far, far away, it turned upwards at right-angles, climbed 100 feet
into the air VERNE struck and killed a dozen birds, and, describing a parabola,
returned to the feet of the hunter red on Lindeman Island you'll be given a
map of walks and a list of birds and plants for you to identify. Take one of
the dinghies across to Royal Seaforth Island and try the fishing over that side
at the end of the world. Take a cruise to other Whitsunday Islands, to the outer
reef (weather permitting), to the underwater observatory at Hook Island, or to
the coral art exhibition on Dent Island—you can do all this from Lindeman
Island red the kangaroo Kandarik on the back of a bark-painting: in the dreamtime he made a wooden drum that was so secret that no woman.
no uninitiated youth was even allowed to hear it, much less to see it. He also
arranged the Ubara ceremony which has to be performed whenever the drum
sounds at the other distant end of the forgotten world. He is wearing a headdress,
and holds between his paws the stick with which he beats the drum. His heart,
lungs, liver and backbone are clearly distinguishable, but the stomach and intestines are replaced by a decorative pattern red on 3 October 1971, Toby Ginger,
his wife and four children on the other side will walk 300 yards across the red
sandy plain on the outskirts of Finke NT near the SA border red back home
at The Antipodes I'm going through the things I've just brought back from
my third trip: two brightly-coloured shirts

PLATYPUS   (0 0)   OPAL   (0 0)   MACROZAMIA   (0 0)   STERN and a pair of pyjamas red in the 19th century governor La Trobe believed there were two kinds of bunyip, northern and southern, and sent his own drawing of the latter to Tasmania where it has unfortunately been lost red to stand off all night not only to avoid the dangers we saw ahead but also to see if there were any other islands. From six to nine o'clock in the evening the water deepened from 14 to 21 fathoms when all at once we fell into 12, ten and eight fathoms. Everyone was at his post. Far, far away. Before ten o'clock we had 20 and 21 fathoms and continued in that depth until a few minutes before 11 o'clock when we had 17, and before we could take another sounding the ship ran hard aground. We immediately took in all our sails, put out the boats and took soundings all around, and found that we had struck the SE edge of a coral reef in no more than three or four fathoms of water in some places round the ship, and in other places a few feet only COOK as soon as the long boat was in the water we struck masts and yards, carried out the stream anchor to starboard, put the coasting anchor and cable into the boat and carried it out to starboard and pulled on it with all our might, which was to no purpose, since the ship was held fast, so we endeavoured to lighten her as fast as possible, which seemed to be the only means of getting her off since we had gone aground at high tide. We sent overboard our iron guns and ballast casks, the jars of oil with wooden hoops, decayed stores red massie = masseuse at the distant end of the forgotten world; bitchie = tart red the people of Wagga Wagga NSW tell how nearly 100 years ago two brothers named Pollman were murdered in their camp on the dunes near Deep Creek, a tributary of the Murrumbidgee River, and their bodies burned. The murderers searched their cart without finding the money which was later discovered by relatives hidden in a cavity in one of the axles at the other end of the world. Some time later a child of ten, who knew nothing of this story, was camping on the same spot with his father, a strapping fellow who was said to fear nothing

LYRE-BIRD   (0 0)   SOUTH   (0 0)   CARBUNCLE   (0 0)   MELALEUCA when the child took over the watch at midnight, for they were travelling with sheep, he went down to the stream to check his fishing lines and heard a cart jolting along the track; whereupon he ran to make a passage through the flock for the travellers, but there was nothing there, not even the horses' hooves, only the sound of squeaking wheels which died away red in 1903 a group of outback workers found black opal, which is very rare and even more beautiful, at Lightning Ridge on the other side of the other end of the world. A great rush ensued; it was the real beginning of opal fever red the next voyage is more famous than any of the preceding ones. Alvaro de Mendoça and Mendaña set out from Peru in 1567 on the other forgotten side of the other end of the vast world without end, discovered the celebrated islands which they named the Solomon Islands on account of their wealth BOUGAINVILLE but even supposing that the detailed accounts of the islands' wealth are not fanciful, their whereabouts is unknown, and they have been sought in vain ever since. All that is known is that they are apparently south of the Line, between the eighth and the 12th parallels. Isle Isabella and the land of Guadalcanal which are mentioned by the same travellers are no better known red the population was controlled, you can read at the Opal Centre far away, by an extremely refined procedure of selective reproduction: marriage to the "correct skin", a practice which not only eliminated inbreeding, but made the Australians the most genetically healthy people in the world red in the subject catalogue: Memoirs of Mrs C. Chisholm with an account of her philanthropic labours in India, Australia, England, to which is added a history of the Family Colonization Loan Society with its rules, regulations and pledges, and also the question answered, who ought to emigrate red by dialling a number in Sydney at the end of the world, you can hear what's on at the city's theatres and cinemas red the terrible mamandi Mamaragan the lightning-man spends the best part of the dry season at the bottom of a waterhole, say the people of Oenpelli at the other end of the world, but he comes out from time to time to gather cabbage-palms

COMPASS   (0 0)   KANGAROO   (0 0)   WESTERN   (0 0)   ELIXIR if ever one of us were to touch the trunk of one of his trees, he would kill him by fire, and if anyone were mad enough to throw a stone into his waterhole, he would rush up into the sky and create such a storm that everyone would be drowned. During the wet season he leaves his home to travel from cloud to cloud. When he becomes angry we hear his rumbling and he throws stone axes which grow out of his hands and knees, spreading terror amongst the slight little mimi and death amongst us red and those of Groote Eylandt believe that a certain number of small stars in our constellation of the Lynx form two celestial scorpions that go hunting in the sky or fishing in the Milky Way, cooking their catch on two large stars nearby, kisses, and that the Sun-woman and her husband once lived in the SE of the island and that when they died their bodies were transformed into two rocks on the shore whilst their souls went up into heaven red continuing with my adventures, Marie-Jo darling: on Wednesday morning I returned to the centre and bought a nice bark painting of a bat from the Aboriginal Affairs shop (my room is not as dull now). MS lent me a light travel bag for what I needed and in the afternoon drove me to the airport. A change at Melbourne, and a journalist and photographer to greet me at Adelaide. Professor D took me to the hotel I had stayed in five years ago, the "Grosvenor" (I've only just realized that it means "great huntsman"), very comfortable with colour TV in the room, but it wasn't much use to me because of the 14 July dinner at the Alliance Française, complete with full-sized guillotine at the door on which the rather merry guests (the wine was flowing freely) were later to guillotine one another with great gusto *austral astronomy* (0 0) LETTERS FROM THE ANTIPODES (0 0) *red NW dream* my grandmother and I are the only survivors of a terrible epidemic of leprosy that leaves us in a sorry state. As I can't stop crying, she tries to console me by making a fishing-line out of her hair, with a bait made out of the lock that looks most like a red feather

NET　　(0 0)　　EMU　　(0 0)　　NEW SOUTH WALES　　(0 0)　　PLASTIC

then I call up out of the water the very first sheets of copper, the protective metal that teaches me the art of hunting. My grandmother dries the meat of the animals I bring her, sews their skins, uses their bones to make many finely sculpted and painted articles, along with wood and copper, and I invite all the people I have met on my expeditions, sing and dance for them, show them the copper and distribute my accumulated wealth to them, especially pieces of the metal in question. I marry two princesses who give me many children showing no traces of the malady I survived; their smell is now delicious, and their skin is as soft, warm and shiny as copper *red NW dream* (o o) LETTERS FROM THE ANTIPODES (o o) *lithographs* Sunday at the diggings as it is sometimes many miles in the interior where the foot of the white man has seldom penetrated, it is not surprising that some time must elapse before a place of worship is built in that imposing style so characteristic of even temporary buildings in Australia, far away; and yet this lack does not prevent one or two good Samaritans from addressing their flock from time to time red the following morning, Marie-Jo darling, the professor of French at the other Adelaide university took me to give a lecture in English at ten o'clock on writing and sexuality. He's a great connoisseur of wine, whisky and French cuisine. Kisses. He wanted to give me some Highland Malt before the lecture, remembering that I'm partial to it (I had already met him on my two previous trips), but it was a little early for me. Then an official luncheon. Then an afternoon with the staff. Then dinner at his place, delicious, copious, the wine was flowing freely red the Tryal Gallery, named after the English ship wrecked on the rocks of Barrow Island in 1622, and the Limmen gallery, after the Dutch ship under Abel Tasman's command during his expedition to the end of the world in 1644 commemorate early visits to WA by English and Dutch sailors: a plate left by Willem de Vlamingh in 1697, and relics from four Dutch vessels wrecked on the coastline

LESCHENAULTIA   (o o)   SCULPTOR   (o o)   OPOSSUM   (o o)   QUEENSLAND

and of the English ship Tryal red the terrible mamandi Wolaundajua the lightning-man, who sleeps during the dry season in a large freshwater pool formed by the river, say the people of Oenpelli at the other end of the vast forgotten world, leaves his lair in the wet season, travelling in the clouds, striking the earth with his long arms, splitting trees and setting light to the grass as he thunders. As for the terrible mamandi Wilintji, in the dreamtime she made her camp at Babanara on the edge of the river, danced all day long and had a hatred of men, whom she trapped and broke their ribs and spinal column with a large stone, then struck them across the nose with a wooden stick until they died. Our ancestors succeeded in surrounding her and spearing her, but she is not quite dead, and wanders around in the guise of a harmless little mimi, claiming she no longer eats anything save nuts from the jungle red and those of Groote Eylandt believe that the three stars of Orion's belt are three fishermen, those of his sword their wives, and that in the dreamtime Jumauria, the Moon-man, had no wife on the other side of the other end of the world, that while travelling in the sky at night he heard a pounding noise and saw the woman Dunaniadmina seated with her family round the fire preparing the evening meal, and that he was so taken with her that he rushed down to Earth and carried her and her family off to the Moon where they can still be made out red on the front of the black and green with a touch of orange $A10 note, next to the plans and facades of a certain number of buildings on the other side of the other end of the world without end, the portrait of Francis Greenway. Nothing on him in the EB. DAB: 1777(?)–1837, architect. Little is known of his childhood and his education. Had a certain reputation at Bristol and Bath in the early 19th century, but went bankrupt in 1811. In 1812 he was in desperate straits, accused of forging part of a contract, and, pleading guilty "on the advice of his friends", was condemned to death. The sentence was commuted to transportation for 14 years

STRAW   (O O)   BORONIA   (O O)   SHIELD   (O O)   ECHIDNA he was a friend of admiral Phillip who was living in retirement in Bath, and who wrote a letter of recommendation to Macquarie on his behalf. Greenway arrived in Sydney in 1814, was soon afterwards placed on parole and immediately began working for the governor. In January 1816 as a civil architect, he was member of a committee charged with making a report on the recently completed house and offices of the secretary general and stated that the building could have been constructed for a third of the sum spent—the beginning of his fight against the corruption common among contractors at the time; in April of the same year he showed Macquarie the necessity of a town plan for Sydney, far away, with provision for a water supply and sewers red by dialling a number in Sydney, far away, you can hear a different chapter of the Bible every morning red in 1579 Pedro Sarmiento, having set out from Callao del Lima with two vessels, was the first person to enter the South Seas by the Strait of Magellan BOUGAINVILLE made some important observations, and on this expedition demonstrated as much courage as intelligence red but with European colonization, you can read at the Opal Centre at the end of the vast forgotten world, it is as much for reasons of health as from the poisonings and massacres that are so often played down or left unmentioned in Australian history books that the Aborigines were almost wiped out like their brothers in Tasmania. Throughout most of the country they have still not recovered from the introduction of new illnesses against which they had no immunity: smallpox, the common cold, eye infections introduced by the Mediterranean fly, venereal diseases and leprosy; it is probably this destruction of health by colonization, as much as malnutrition, which has resulted in the Aborigines today having the highest infantile mortality rate in the world red the people of Wonganilla and Pine Ridge VIC tell how in a village named Trotting Cob at the other end of the world, a horseman appears each night with his head under his arm red after QLD and NSW the fabulous stone was found in a third state

TASMANIA   (O O)   BARK   (O O)   ISOPOGON   (O O)   TELESCOPE

in 1915 at the foot of a long winding cliff West of Lake Eyre in SA on the
other side of the other end of the world, two gold prospectors set up camp
one night, and the next day collected a hatful of opals—beginning a new rush
red fortunately we had little wind and fine weather with a calm sea for 24
hours. At nine o'clock the ship righted herself, but the pumps were no longer
able to contain the leak. This was a terrible danger which threatened to destroy
us as soon as the ship was afloat. So I risked all and decided to raise her,
and consequently I put on the capstans all hands that were not employed on
the pumps, and at about twenty past ten the ship was afloat in deep water
on the other side of the other end of the world without end. Then I sent the
long boat to look for the main anchor; it found it, but lost the cable among
the rocks COOK at 11 o'clock we got under sail and headed towards land with
a light ESE breeze, some hands were employed in stemming the leak with a
sail stuffed with wool, others continued to pump red golfie = golf player, far
away; bowlie = bowls player (minimum age 60) red back home at The Antipodes:
stickers, unused Bank of NSW chequebook, far, far away, a bottle of optazine
(eye-drops), a tube of Uncle Sam toothpaste with stars and stripes red the Wagga
Wagga NSW paper reports the appearance of a bunyip in a lagoon on 13 April
1872 at the end of the world: one and a half times the size of a dog, covered
with very black, shiny, long hair, twenty centimetres of it, completely hiding
his eyes red on the back of an X-ray style bark painting: black kangaroo speared
by a hunter, with the large body, powerful tail and hind legs contrasting with
the small head, slender neck and shoulders and feeble forelegs at the other
end of the world. The spine is shown clearly because it supports the whole body,
likewise the femora

DRAGON LIZARD   (0 0)   NORTHERN TERRITORY   (0 0)   PAPER   (0 0)   CROTALARIA the lungs, liver and intestines can also be made out. The figure of the hunter is full of movement. His bag is dangling from his neck. Warraguk, my bat, is painted in the same style. Although his head is in profile, the two eyes are shown red on 3 October 1971 Toby Ginger is going to leave his hessian and corrugated iron hut for a new house, a house that is not just thrown down onto the edge of the Simpson Desert by the giant white hand of a faraway government on the other side of the other end of the world, but a house which he, a member of the Apatula group of the Pitjantjatjara tribe has helped design, constructed for the Aboriginal Housing Society of which he is a member by members of the Apatula group red Glenarvan and his companions were stunned; they couldn't believe their eyes on the other side of the other dazzling end of the forgotten world without end. "It's the boomerang!" said Ayrton. "The boomerang! cried Paganel VERNE the Australian boomerang!" And like a child, he went and picked up the marvellous instrument to see what was inside it red take a trip in our glass-bottomed boat and admire the coral reefs at Lindeman Island, play billiards or table-tennis in the recreation room far away, talk over a quiet drink in the glassed-in bar which overlooks Kennedy Sound and Royal Seaforth Island, take a light plane trip over the Whitsunday Islands, the Outer Reef and on to Brampton Island—and then after dinner, two nights a week, there's music in the bar or outside, with full-length movies once a week, party-night on Monday, games on other nights—you're going to love Lindeman Island red in the 14th century, on the wall of my room in college, a new wave of Polynesians arrived in New Zealand, bringing an agricultural civilization. They formed an aristocracy. By the time that contacts with the Europeans had become regular, at the end of the 18th century, the Maoris were skilled farmers. Far, far away. They often traded in the ports of call of merchant or whaling vessels, and in the small settlements of Australian whalers that grew up towards 1820

TRIANGLE   (0 0)   PLATYPUS   (0 0)   VICTORIA   (0 0)   WOOD trade and agriculture remained the country's principal activities after the British conquest. Britain, in spite of her entry into the Common Market, remains its most important trading partner. Meat, wood and dairy produce. Tiki (little green jade statue with its head on one side and big eyes). Maori tattooing. Maori craftsmen are skilled woodcarvers. Canoe dance red Michael knows all the secrets, all the ins and outs of male massage, come and find out, at the end of the world; mystic massage $A15, join our club for big reductions, ask for Terry, Jackie or Jo; Tricia's, the house of sophistication, ultra-modern studio with girls specializing in French, correct Spanish and herbal foam massage, discretion assured, two girl massage, five girls to choose from who are ready for anything and will give you that little extra; Mandy's, we're new, we'll take the time to spoil you, low, low prices, mmmarvellous massages, such understanding girls, and a very discreet location red when one of us dies, say the people of Yirrkala, kisses, while the women are transferring his bones from one coffin to the other, the men perform the water dance. The sister of the deceased or his closest cousin digs a hole in the ground, the coffin is placed in it in an upright position, the earth packed round its base, the small bones of his hands and feet distributed to friends and relations, his skull broken up and the pieces scattered to the winds red how do the Aborigines trade? All kinds of goods: pigments, implements, weapons, ornaments, sacred objects, are traded along well defined trade routes, some of which cross the entire continent. The exchange of gifts is an important part of economic, social and ritual life. Pearl shells worn by initiated men and used in magic come from the NW coast and sometimes travel more than a thousand miles, like the hollow shells made into scoops or ornaments on the coastal areas of Cape York. Stone axes, quartz knives are an important currency

REGELIA   (0 0)   TOUCAN   (0 0)   LYRE-BIRD   (0 0)   BRICK the narcotic called pitjuri comes from a plant that grows in the SW of QLD; its stems and leaves are chopped into tiny pieces and wrapped in special sacks; it is chewed by many tribes in the interior. Ochre is also a currency. Songs and dances are exchanged at gatherings. Boomerangs made in the Centre and in the North are found everywhere. Arnhem Land tribes that do not make them procure them for use as musical instruments *Unesco exhibition* (o o) LETTERS FROM THE ANTIPODES (o o) *showbag* in August each year the city of Brisbane experiences the great excitement of the QLD show: merry-go-rounds, rodeos, wood-chopping competitions, and above all wool, banana, forest products, sugar-cane and agricultural machinery stands, stands for everything. Each stand offers for a few cents a paper bag called a "showbag" filled with advertising samples which children adore. There is no difficulty where biscuits are concerned, but for example every bank offers bags which take a little more imagination. As I left, I returned to the respective people who had lent them, and in particular to MS, the articles which had helped me to survive, and gave the whole the title of Brisbane Kit or Writer's in Residence Showbag, in seven provinces and three territories, together with a little index on modified postcards, originally purchased at Surfer's Paradise and still in their yellow bag entitled Souvenirs of Paradise, which I had also modified slightly by adding the two handles necessary for its new function. The first card bears the title and dedication to MS, along with the caption: Surfers Paradise QLD, surf beach on the Gold Coast with the MacPherson Range behind red what are the religious beliefs of the Aborigines? The ancestors of the dreamtime include the Fertility Mother and other mythical women of Arnhem Land, great snake ancestors in the Kimberleys and the rest of the NT, bands of human and animal totemic spirits in the Centre and sky-heroes in the East. Kisses. Their lives and activities as modellers of the present-day world, its inhabitants, animals and plants, its tribal customs, are re-enacted in narrative ceremonies

BEAUFORTIA   (o o)   SAILS   (o o)   KANGAROO   (o o)   SOUTH youths are initiated into the beliefs, rites, codes of discipline and behaviour maintained by the elders, undergo the ordeal by fire and ritual operations such as tooth-extraction and circumcision, sometimes subincision. The bull-roarer whose buzzing is the voice of the ancestors warns away the women and the uninitiated. Everybody assembles in a large circle around the dance-site, but only the initiates and novitiates go along the path to the small sacred circle where the ceremonies take place red massage parlours are supposed to be forbidden in QLD, but you only have to read the personal column of the Courier-Mail, Saturday 10 July 1976 for example: AAAAAAsk for a star, star hostesses; what are you thinking about Irene, what are you reading? AAAAArabella, hostess for all occasions, far, far away; AAA Chantel's, escorts available; AAAtractive young woman, 36, wanting a little more out of life, very few friends at present, spends most of her time at home, seeks virile understanding man; AA Ladies, are you lonely? Whether you're a single mother, pregnant and unmarried, unattached, divorced or widowed, we have many virile men throughout the State who want your company red when one of us dies, once his wooden coffin has been placed in its final position and everyone has returned home, what are you dreaming about Mathilde, where are you, what are you reading? say the people of Yirrkala at the end of the world, his soul is at last separated from his bones, and if he belongs to the dua moiety of his tribe, he enters a bark canoe paddled by the soul of the first man to die and goes towards Junundi, a jungle on the west shore of Melville Bay where he is met by the angels whom the archangels Wuluwait and Bunbulama have brought together in his honour red South Molle is where the good old days still are and where you ought to be. You'll live on the edge of a long, white beach and fill your days with water sports, golf, tennis, walks at the other end of the dazzling forgotten world, happy days and swinging nights on South Molle Island red a political map of the Pacific at the beginning of the 16th century would have shown hundreds of kingdoms in Micronesia and Polynesia

STONE   (0 0)   CALOTHAMNOS   (0 0)   FLYING FISH   (0 0)   EMU thousands of little independent communities in Melanesia and in Australia. War-fare was common, island empires rose and fell with the tide of battle, further round the map on the wall of my room in college on the other side of the other end of the world, the Europeans introduced firearms along with Chris-tianity, with catastrophic results in certain areas. In the 19th century the mis-sionaries attempted to reduce the slaughter by supporting the rise of powerful chiefs for whom they drafted laws, for example Taufa'ahau who became king of Tonga in 1862 and adopted a constitution. Apart from Spanish possessions in Micronesia and English colonies in Australia, European imperialism did not begin to invade the Pacific until the 19th century when settlers began to find that native governments were incapable of satisfying their demands for political stability, land and work. France, Germany, Great Britain and the United States intervened to protect their citizens' interests, and by the end of the century Europe and America controlled the entire ocean red Toby Ginger's house and the five other ones to be built are flexible instruments for helping a people who have been nomadic since the dreamtime on the other side of the other end of the world without end, and who are now forced to stay put red the boomerang simply consisted of a piece of hard, curved wood, from 30 to 40 inches long. Its thickness in the middle was around three inches, far away, and its two ends terminated in sharp points VERNE its concave part went in some six inches and its convex part had two very sharp edges. It was as simple as it was incomprehensible red in 1873 the Wagga Wagga NSW Express reported that a bunyip had been seen twice in three months in Cowal Lake, far, far away, with the head of an old Aborigine with long black hair red the friendly spirit called Ingwalin on the back of a bark painting: thin, tall, hairless body, head covered by a mop of long hair, a fan made of feathers in one hand

WESTERN   (0 0)   BANDICOOT   (0 0)   COPPER   (0 0)   WARATAH

in the other a club with which he drives away evil spirits at the end of the
dazzling forgotten world, pays frequent visits to the graves of the dead, tries
in vain to make them stand up red cosie = bathing costume at the other end
of the world; nightie = nightdress red back home at The Antipodes: bark painting representing Warraguk the bat; a magic spike and a forehead band from
Mornington Island; some banksia, African tulip and Chinese gooseberry seeds;
a spear tip made of white glass, a grass-string bag from Milingimbi red the opal
field found by the O'Neil brothers was named Coober Pedy by the Aborigines
on the other side of the other end of the world, which means Whites in a hole
red sent the quartermaster along with two boats to take soundings around the
ship on the other side of the other end of the world without end, and find
a port where we might make the repairs necessary to put the ship into proper
trim COOK at eight o'clock one of the boats returned to report that they had
found one red anthropologists can do no more than estimate the population
before colonization, you can read at the Opal Centre, far away, but to get an
idea of the extent of the extermination one should remember that the most
heavily populated regions were along the coast where the Whites are concentrated today red the people of Queanbeyan NSW tell how on 28 June 1876 a
shepherd named McCarthy had been murdered at a spot called Washpen near
Yeumbra on the Murrumbidgee river. The police discovered that his body had
been buried at the entrance to his log cabin. Far, far away. A verdict was brought
in of murder by person or persons unknown red by dialling a number in Sydney
at the end of the world, you can gear the gospel for the day red in 1595, Alvaro
de Mendaña who had been on the voyage of Mendoça in the year 1567, set
out again from Peru with four ships in search of the Solomon Islands

AIR PUMP   (0 0)   OPOSSUM   (0 0)   SOUTH WALES   (0 0)   KOALA discovered between the ninth and 11th parallel south, around 108°W of Paris, the isles of San Pedro, Magdalena, Dominica and Saint Christina which he named the Marquesas of Mendoça after Dona Isabella de Mendoça who was on the voyage BOUGAINVILLE around 24° further to the West he discovered the Isle of San Bernando; almost 200 leagues to the West of these the Solitary Isle, and finally the Isle of Santa Cruz situated around 140°E of Paris. The fleet then sailed to the Mariana Islands and finally on to the Philippines where General Mendaña failed to arrive; it is not known what happened to his ship red the people of Groote Eylandt believe that when the tides are at their highest the sea rises up to the Moon and fills it and that is why it is round, white or ash-grey, that at neap tide the seawater runs out of the Moon, leaving it thin, that the Magellan Clouds are the camp of an old man and an old woman who are so feeble that they cannot find their own food, but that the other inhabitants of the sky bring them fish and bulbs which they cook on their fire red the first Australian architect in the subject catalogue on the other red side of the other end of the forgotten world without end, in the collection Australian Landmarks where you can also find: the Aboriginal Australians, the Sydney Gazette, Enter the Squatter, Fencing Australia, Early Australian Women, Enter the Merchant, Tall Ships and Steamboats, Exploring the Air; school books with topics to be done: 1) look at the illustrations of Greenway's buildings, or visit at least one original, then look at modern structures; which type of architecture do you prefer and why? 2) if Greenway were alive today he would definitely be in Who's Who in Australia, which you can find in any public library. Read the biography of some well known living person, the prime minister, or the leader of the opposition, or perhaps a famous architect, then write Greenway's in the same style, 3) from this work or from others mentioned in the bibliography reconstruct a day in the life of Greenway red in the Cygnet gallery, named after the English ship of William Dampier who landed at Cape Leveque in 1688

SILVER   (O O)   ANIGOSANTHOS   (O O)   BIRD OF PARADISE   (O O)   ECHIDNA you can see the establishment of the Swan River colony in 1829, far away, with Fremantle as the first permanent British settlement in WA red the rainbow-serpent Ngaloit lives at the bottom of a waterhole formed by Fish Creek, say the people of Oenpelli far, far away, he is brilliantly-coloured, with long whiskers and long teeth. If children come to bathe in his waterhole, he sends little snakes after them which enter their navel and cause their death red the lost bushman or the unfortunate prospector who never returned: no pen could adequately convey the terror, the savage emotion ending in the deepest melancholic depression, of one who, having attempted in vain to retrace his steps, realizes that he is lost. How many whose names appear in every number of the Melbourne Argus under the heading "missing friends" lie bleaching in the virgin bush: the burning sun poured on his weakened frame/no kindly spirit standing at his side/without a slab to mark his name/the famished lost one in the prairie died red more was to come on Friday at the University of Adelaide, Marie-Jo darling: lecture in French on travel and writing at 11 o'clock, official luncheon, then a walk in the city with a lady who's doing a thesis on Passing Time, whom I'd asked to go with me to an Aboriginal art shop to buy a grass-string bag from Arnhem Land; repeat lecture in English on writing and sexuality, and I was forgetting a radio interview just before lunch; two short hours, break for studying the local paper and in particular the small ads, then an official dinner given by the vice-chancellor; I only had one thing in mind, to go off to bed, all the more because the next day we were supposed to leave early for the mountains; and then I had forgotten the visit before the morning lecture to the new Adelaide Festival Centre, a remarkable collection of concert halls and theatres with works of art of a very high standard *lithographs* (0 0) LETTERS FROM THE ANTIPODES (0 0) *gaps* the first that come to mind: gold, the conveniences and their graffiti

QUEENSLAND   (0 0)   BARRAMUNDI   (0 0)   PEARL   (0 0)   CEPHALOTUS the lost treasures, the extent of the desert red the next day, Saturday the D's took me to the Flinders Ranges, Marie-Jo darling; they'd taken two extra pullovers for me which came in handy. Kisses. The town spread out like American suburbia, then we crossed some very flat plains covered with sheep, went through the little town of Clare with its vineyards and arrived at the foot of the first mountain which is called the Remarkable. The range isn't high and the summit is only 1,170 m, but it's extremely steep and jagged. We picnicked by a creek in the delightful village of Melrose with its old verandahed houses and hotels. Then we went through a gorge and found ourselves on a coastal plain where we got lost. After an hour it became clear that we were following the gorge we had just been through in the opposite direction; a loop of 100 km. At last we got back on the right road and the landscape became more and more wild and uneven; one advantage of our lateness was that we had to cross this extraordinary area at twilight on the other side of the other end of the world without end. An emu said good evening to us as we passed, and we arrived at the hotel in the dark just in time for dinner; it was comfortable, the waitresses charming, but the rooms had only one tiny electric radiator that was quite inadequate for the temperature which had suddenly dropped. Luckily I was in a twin-bedded room and I put all the blankets on mine. JD had asked me to wake him at seven o'clock the next morning if I could manage so that we could take a walk at daybreak before breakfast. I made myself a cup of tea and put on my pullovers, all four layers. The car windows were covered in ice; a quick scrape, and we set off for the entrance of what is known as Wilpena Pound; it's an inverted relief: because of erosion, the floor of a valley—a basin—is now higher than the surrounding area. It's what you might call a concave mesa

ALTAR   (0 0)   DRAGON LIZARD   (0 0)   TASMANIA   (0 0)   WOMBAT the edges are very steep brown and red rocky cliffs, and inside there's a kind of remarkably impregnable Garden of Eden, with the only way in along a very narrow path beside a creek. A kangaroo of fairly small stock, as tall as a child of ten, known as an "euro", took a long look at us before slipping away without haste, some emus red the first part of the showbag is called tucker-box in memory of the tin which the outback vagabonds called swagmen carried with them for use as a food container; it lists all the food we had left over. What are you eating, Irène, what are you looking at, where are you? The caption of the card which is dedicated to QLD and the opossum has: ripe bunch of bananas; they are picked when still green because they travel best in this condition. Far away. At their destination, they finish ripening in dark, warm, humid warehouses. They are grown commercially from Coff's Harbour NSW to Cairns QLD and in tropical and subtropical areas of WA red the female rainbow-serpent Narama who lives with her sons among the rocks on the shore at the mouth of the river, what are you eating Mathilde, what are you dreaming about, say the people of Oenpelli, far, far away, is brilliantly-coloured, has large ears and a beard, hates us and if one of us goes near her lair, she bites his spirit and causes him to die, makes a sniffling noise, then rises into the sky to form a rainbow and make clouds and rain red a new "rush" created by the discovery of gold; the rumours quickly spread and most of the locals leave home and hurry to the new mine. It is amusing and terribly instructive to see many thousands of men, women and children gathering at the spot where gold is known to have been found, with only a blanket and a piece of tent-cloth to cover them at the end of the world. All those who go on the rush take a swag (bundle of clothes), a billy (round kettle), a tomahawk (pick), a tent, and in a very short time the uninhabited desert becomes a densely-populated town red on the back of the $A10 note, next to the buildings of an outback township

CORAL   (O O)   BUNYA   (O O)   GRAVING-TOOL   (O O)   PLATYPUS and a profusion of flourishes the portrait of Henry Lawson. EB: 1867–1922, author of bitter-sweet short stories and ballads, born 17 June New Grenfell NSW, father a Norwegian sailor turned goldminer called Larsen who changed his name upon registering his son's birth at the other dazzling end of the red world. The family moved to Eurunderee where he began school, then to Mudgee. He was partially deaf and his private life was a constant struggle against poverty and domestic problems. Left school at 14 to help his father who was working as a mason, moved to Sydney around 1844 and published his first verses and first short story in the Bulletin, worked on the Brisbane Boomerang for six months in 1890 and on the Sydney Worker in '92. Worked as housepainter, sawmill worker, telegraph linesman, teacher in a Maori school in New Zealand, also a bush vagabond (swagman); his vivid, bold work, containing both pathos and irony, captures an essential aspect of Australian life. A visit to England in 1900 had disastrous consequences. He separated from his wife whom he had married in '96 and his last years were increasingly unhappy in spite of financial help from his publishers and a small pension red in the Geelvinck gallery, named after a Dutch vessel in which Willem de Vlamingh explored the coast in '97 from the Swan River, which he thus named, to the NW Cape while searching for another ship lost in 1685 on the other side of the other end of the world, furniture, household utensils and other articles brought out by early colonists red Fernando de Quiros, a companion of the ill-fated Mendaña, and who had brought Donna Isabella back to Peru, set out from there again with two vessels on 21 December 1605 and set an approximate WSW course. First he discovered a small island about 25°S and 124°W of Paris, and named it the Isle of Beautiful People on the other side of the other end of the world without end. While subsequently searching for the Isle of Santa Cruz which he had seen on his first voyage, a search that was fruitless, he discovered at 13°S and about 176°E of Paris the Isle of Taumaco

NORTHERN TERRITORY   (0 0)   GOANNA   (0 0)   RUBY   (0 0)   BLACK BOY then around 100 leagues to the West of that island at 15°S a large land which he named the Southern Land of the Holy Spirit, and which various geographers have situated in various places BOUGAINVILLE there he finished running Westward and rejoined the route to Mexico where he arrived at the end of 1606 after having again sought in vain the Isle of Santa Cruz red the people of Groote Eylandt believe that two brothers would often come and tickle a cod living beneath a rock in a lagoon and admire its size, with the intention of killing it one day, but that the fish, which had grown enormous, caught hold of their hands and dragged them into the water and ate them far away, and that he then left the lagoon for the sea, creating some rivers, and met two rainbow-serpents and made his camp near theirs, but that the two dead men's brothers came and killed him, that his body has become a large rock and that his spirit has gone swimming in the sky where he has become what we call the Coal Sack in the Milky Way, and that he was speared by the spirits of the two brothers whom he had swallowed, who are two of the stars in our Southern Cross, who divided him and cooked half on each fire, forming two other stars, and that near the brothers are their two avengers, two stars of our Centaur constellation who sing and strike their boomerangs red the people of Queanbeyan tell how the police set about finding the murderer and that in a creek bed not far from the hut they found some strange footprints made by someone with two left boots. They were very clear and led to the home of the settler who employed the victim, far, far away. When he learned of the murder he at once suggested that the person responsible was one Tom the Soldier or Waterloo Tom red by dialling a number in Sydney at the end of the forgotten red world, you can hear the prayer for the day red made our ship fast in the port at the other end of the world COOK and pulled it up onto a fairly steep beach on the southern shore red the only increase in the number of black people in Australia for which Europeans are responsible was on the QLD coast where during the last century planters

KEEL   (0 0)   LYRE-BIRD   (0 0)   VICTORIA   (0 0)   DUGONG brought slaves from the West Pacific, you can read at the Opal Centre on the other side of the other end of the world, but these people from Micronesia and Melanesia are related to the Torres Strait people and to the former inhabitants of Tasmania red back home at The Antipodes: O'Reilly's Green Mountains, tourist track map of the Lamington National Park (fragment) on the other side of the other end of the world without end; Total map of NSW, of QLD red when Coober Pedy was discovered, superior quality opals were selling for between three and five pounds an ounce. The mine has turned out to be the biggest in the world, far away, yielding far more opals than any other red Bubba Peibi on the back of a bark painting: short and fat, only two and a half feet high, he holds a long fishing spear for catching fish at night, which he puts in his basket or drags through the water by a line threaded round their gills far, far away. He lives inside a banyan tree and can enlarge his entrance hole by blowing on it, and makes his fire there to cook his fish on; he can only be seen by our medicine-men who need to keep a close eye on him so that there is a little fish left over for the rest of us red cookie = biscuit at the end of the world; woolie = pullover red so this is the famous boomerang! said Paganel when he had closely examined the bizarre instrument. A piece of wood and nothing else at the other end of the world. Why, when it is flying horizontally VERNE does it suddenly climb into the sky and return to the hand that threw it? Scientists and travellers have never been able to explain the phenomenon. "Wouldn't the effect be like that of a hoop which, if thrown in a certain way, returns to its point of departure?" said John Mangles. "Or rather," added Glenarvan, "like putting bottom on a billiard ball when you strike it on a certain part?" "Not at all," replied Paganel, "in these two cases, there is a point of contact which determines the reaction; the ground for the hoop, the cloth for the billiard ball

SAPPHIRE　　(O O)　　EUCALYPTUS　　(O O)　　CENTAUR　　(O O)　　KANGAROO but in this case there is no point of contact, the instrument doesn't touch the ground, and yet it climbs to a considerable height red the reverend Taplin, in his book on the Narrinyeri on the other side of the other end of the world, tells how he often heard explosive and booming sounds on Lake Alexandrina and that the Aborigines explained to him that it was the bunyip red after Spain's defeat in the Spanish-American war in 1898 on the wall of my room in college, Germany and the United States shared its former possessions in Micronesia. After the first world war, Australia, New Zealand and Japan annexed German territories in New Guinea, Samoa and Micronesia on the other side of the other inverted end of the forgotten world without end. The Japanese extended their zone of influence in the second. After '45 control of the Pacific became primarily the responsibility of the United States and Great Britain. France retained its overseas departments and territories. Most countries are seeking independence, with Samoa obtaining it in '62, Nauru in '68, Fiji and Tonga in '70, Papua-New Guinea in '75. Maori war canoe, with its sculpted prow jutting into the map red when Toby Ginger and his family set out on their long walk on 3 October '71, they are not going to move into the house itself, but into the courtyard surrounded by a brick wall five feet high. Far away. The top rows will be of open bricks so that the family squatting round the fire will not feel too closed-in and will be able to see what is going on outside if they straighten up red when one of us dies, say the people of Yirrkala, far, far away, after he arrives at the jungle of the angels, he dances all night with his hands full of flowers red Happy Bay on Long Island, the place to unwind. Your beachfront cabin is surrounded by swaying palms, with miles of blue water stretching out before you at the end of the world—get away from it all at Happy Bay red what is the ceremonial life of the Aborigines? Feathered design from Central Australia; kisses; liturgical ceremony in Arnhem Land

TURTLE   (O O)   GOLD   (O O)   WATTLE   (O O)   CHAMELEON decorating the totemic chief, Central Australia, in order to increase the totem species; swinging the bull-roarer; beating the ubar, Arnhem Land, with the sound of the gong representing the voice of a snake ancestor; dance of the Wawalag sisters, mythical ancestors of many Arnhem Land groups, associated with many sites; turkey dance, Northern Territory; kangaroo dance, Central Australia; women decorated for an erotic dance; ground figure, Central Australia, made from red and white down stuck down with human blood, marking the site of important events in the dreamtime; corroboree with boomerangs, QLD red Angelic Escorts for pleasant, refined company; attractive, lively companions for out-of-town visitors, ask for Capricorn hostesses; attractive, broad-minded couple, early 30's, would like to meet pleasant, educated and broad-minded people for friendship, possible swinging; Ladies and Gentlemen, don't remain on your own, join our golden circle for future friendships, hundreds of addresses, no fee for ladies; business couple, both very attractive, under 30, seek attractive, broad-minded girl for fun times, discretion assured, send photo *small ads* (o o) LETTERS FROM THE ANTIPODES (o o) *children's drawings* Tonni has painted where he lives as a large red and orange expanse with humps. An enormous yellow Sun is consuming the earth. A horseman is riding hard into the bottom left-hand corner, leaving a shallow track in the sand red attractive, vivacious divorcee seeks business man for mutual arrangements, relax and enjoy leisure times in my company and my surroundings; attractive, fun-loving business couple, 25, living on the Gold Coast, seek similar couple for friendship and possible swinging; kisses; good-looking, good-natured guy, would like to meet chick, the same, for fun times, photo if possible; British widow, 47, charming personality, seeks gentleman companion of any nationality to give her life more meaning, contact Lola Introductions red the shop at Happy Bay on Long Island stocks chemist lines

EMU　　(o o)　　SOUTH　　(o o)　　KOOKABURRA　　(o o)　　PLATINUM

photographic supplies, clothing, shell jewellery, confectionery, free laundry, sick bay, bank agencies, mail three times a week. What are you looking at, Cécile, where are you, what are you reading, far, far away? The shop has stamps, there are telegram facilities, Brisbane papers, a safe for valuables, 240 volt electricity, running water everywhere—do as you please at Happy Bay red what are the features of Aboriginal medicine? What are you looking at, Agnès, what are you eating? Sorcerers kill or blind their victims after capturing their spirit, which is in their hair or their food, by means of chants and by casting a spell on them with a pointing-bone, which is then burnt or buried at the end of the world; the only hope of recovery lies in finding where it has gone through the counter-magic of a more powerful medicine-man. The Central Australian sorcerer uses shoes made of emu-feathers stuck together with human blood to erase his footprints. Quartz and other crystals symbolize the magic power of causing death and bringing on or curing illness, bringing rain or causing people to fall in love. Pebbles, shells including pearl-shells, and ornaments are used in magic. Medicine-men effect cures by extracting a piece of quartz, bone or coagulated bad blood from the painful part of the body, which they massage and suck. Wounds are covered with a poultice made of clay, or of blood, fat and perspiration; medicinal plants are used, and preventive charms are worn. Rites bring rain to freshen the countryside, reveal the tracks of game, conceal the tracks of a criminal or augment the water supply. Divination rites are performed at tombs to discover those responsible for the killing red when Toby Ginger's family feels at its ease, they will move into the only room in the house at the other inverted end of the forgotten world. When they are used to it and can keep it clean, the walls can be shifted to make two bedrooms red when one of us dies, once he has danced all night with the angels, say the people of Yirrkala on the other side of the other end of the world, he and his boatman, accompanied by dolphins, leave for the Island of Dambalia where they dance through the following night, their hands full of red yam flowers red W. Westgarth in Australia Felix (1848) describes the bunyip as an enormous animal

BANKSIA   (o o)   COMPASS   (o o)   OPOSSUM   (o o)   WESTERN

with a round head, on the other side of the other end of the world without
end, a long neck and a body and tail resembling an ox red from the depths
of the Pacific volcanic activity has pushed up many mountain ranges, further
round the map. Some of their peaks emerge through the water. Far away. In
the tropics small lime-monitoring animals and plants attach themselves to the
sides of peaks such as those in Fiji or Hawaii, just beneath sea level, creating
a fringe of coral. If the ocean floor sinks this coastal reef becomes a barrier,
then an atoll like those of the Gilbert and Ellice archipelagoes. The Australian
Great Barrier Reef, 2,000 km long, includes thousands of these different kinds
of reefs, formed by at least 350 different species of coral red pantie = women's
knickers far, far away, girdie = women's corset red so how do you explain
this fact, Monsieur Paganel?" asked Lady Helena. "I am not explaining it,
Madam, I am stating it once again at the inverted end of the forgotten world;
the effect obviously results from the way the boomerang is thrown and its special
construction VERNE but, as to the manner of throwing, that's still the secret
of the Australians!" "At all events, it's very ingenious . . . for apes," added Lady
Helena, looking at the major, who shook his head, unconvinced red while Coober
Pedy was being developed, the Lightning Ridge rush had produced a large quantity of black opals at the other end of the world, in 1918 the price had gone
up to two pounds a carat for a good quality stone red general initiation on
the back of a bark painting: the initiate is circumcised while lying on the backs
of prone men forming an operating table, becoming a Lurugu, followed by a
subincision when he will become a Waramma; he will have to learn a special
language called Darin containing nasal sounds which are found only among
the Aborigines and the Boshimans on the other side of the other end of the
world. Surrounding scenes include: corroboree (tribal gathering dance), fishing

BUNYIP   (0 0)   DIAMOND   (0 0)   CLIANTHUS   (0 0)   DOVE sting-ray with barbs that are pulled out for use as circumcision instruments red for a long time the formula "divide and rule" was applied to the Aborigines and Islanders of QLD, you can read at the Opal Centre on the other side of the other end of the world without end, a great differentiation was made between pure blood and half-caste; but we, the Aborigines of today, the descendants of both, are united in being black red back home at The Antipodes: Free Guide to Toowoomba and the Darling Downs, bark painting labels from the Department of Aboriginal Affairs shop red by dialling a number in Sydney, far, far away, you can hear the recipe of the day red yesterday evening we put ashore our provisions and a large part of our reserves at the end of the world, landed our sick COOK set up the forge and installed the armourer and his mate to make nails etc. to repair the ship red the people of Groote Eylandt believe that the Milky Way is a river flowing in the sky with no fish in its waters, no birds flying above it at the other end of the world, covered in waterlilies whose bulbs are the food of the sky-dwellers, and that alongside there grows a large plum tree red the people of Queanbeyan also tell how the farmer told the police that Waterloo Tom had knocked on his door on the eve of the crime, and that he had given him a bed, that Tom had asked him if the shepherd McCarthy was still occupying his hut and that he had said yes on the other side of the other end of the world, that the next day he had been relieved to find that he had gone, in spite of the fact that he had stolen a blanket, a canister containing strychnine and a left boot, how Waterloo Tom was arrested red in the Discovery Gallery, named after the English ship in which George Vancouver visited the southern coast of WA in 1791 on the other unknown side of the other distant end of the world without end during his voyage round the world, you can see various aspects of life in old Fremantle: enlargements of old photographs and advertisements, dresses, household utensils red Abel Tasman left Batavia on 14 August 1642, and discovered at 42°S and around 155°E of Paris a land far away which he named Van Diemen

ECHIDNA   (0 0)   NEW SOUTH WALES   (0 0)   COCKATOO   (0 0)   OPAL he went on and travelled East, and around 160° of our eastern longitude, he discovered New Zealand at 42°10′S BOUGAINVILLE he followed its coast down to 34°S whence he steered NE and discovered at 22°35′ around 174°E of Paris the islands of Pylstaart, Amsterdam and Rotterdam. He did not pursue his explorations any further and returned to Batavia by passing between New Guinea and Gilolo red concert at a new gold-mine in Australia: a rather primitive spectacle, the prospectors want some amusement after their day's work far, far away, they love rough and ready bars, shows of this kind are very much in vogue, especially on recent diggings red DAB: Signed Henry Lawson at the end of the world. His father, Peter Jertzberg Larsen, was a Norwegian sailor, a well-informed man who appreciated the poetry of the Old Testament but could barely write, and who tried his fortunes on various goldfields and then moved to Pipeclay NSW, now Eurunderee where he met Louisa Albury, the daughter of a carpenter and married her on 7 July 1866; he was 32, she 18. After bringing up the children, she played an important part in feminist movements and edited a women's paper called Dawn from May 1888 to July 1905; she also published the first volume by her son who thought he had inherited gypsy blood through her. After his birth near Grenfell the family returned to Eurunderee where the father took up a selection, but little could be done with the poor land red the third card is about the second province of the Brisbane kit: cutlery and crockery, dedicated to the NT and the dragon lizard at the other end of the world. Caption: Australian Aboriginal, made in West Germany red one day in the dreamtime two of our ancestors were hunting at Kabawudnar near the bay, say the people of Oenpelli on the other distant side of the other end of the unknown world, when they saw an emu, not realizing it was Gurugadji: they succeeded in catching it, one by the neck, the other by the head, but Gurugadji managed to escape and, plunging into a waterhole, transformed himself into a rainbow-serpent which swallowed them red and there will also be at least a few lines missing on Mark Twain and Australia

HAKEA (0 0) SOUTHERN CROSS (0 0) DRAGON LIZARD (0 0) QUEENSLAND the shells and the coral, kisses, the English painter John Glover who came to settle in TAS in 1831 at the age of 64 and died there at 83, the trees in the desert red we almost got lost again in the morning while visiting two superb gorges, Marie-Jo darling, then we picked up the road after lunch, and this time we definitely went through the pass we had missed the previous day, famed in Australian tourism for its delightful narrow-gauge railway which has just been restored and operates twice a week in season. For some years it went as far as Alice Springs. We made a detour to Port Augusta, the most southerly point on the gulf, and on the dividing line between cultivated land and desert, with its Aborigines who come in for provisions, then we came back along the sea by national route 1 which goes almost round Australia (there's still a section missing in the North between Darwin and Cairns). Now and again there were pretty farms in the countryside, surrounded by clumps of trees standing out against the vastness of the fields or the meadows; a colonial house with its verandah on all sides, shelters for the animals covered with straw; sometimes a mass of cockatoos would sweep down; there can be a thousand or more, so that it seems that the branches have just blossomed with magnificent white flowers; this can even happen right on campus at the University of QLD, I saw it yesterday afternoon. Approaching Adelaide it was completely dark, and the traffic got denser; the return from the weekend. Next morning JD drove me to the airport for the seven o'clock flight; he had spent his weekend driving 1,200 km for my enjoyment. Before I left I had asked MS if I could bring him something back from Adelaide where he spent his first years in Australia; he asked me for a pot of Fauchon mustard; the professor at Flinders University had a whole stock in his cellar; so throughout the expedition I went everywhere with a large sandstone pot in my bag *gaps* (o o) LETTERS FROM THE ANTIPODES (o o) *free hand* the eye that is neither forewarned, that is, not instructed about what it is about to see, nor has its vision impaired by the Western "manner of seeing" with which it has been invested for centuries, has only to travel over these Arnhem Land bark paintings

WALLABY   (O O)   CARBUNCLE   (O O)   GREVILLEA   (O O)   CROW to be rewarded, first, by their exemplary harmony BRETON well before it discerns the intentions that lie behind them, it will be enraptured by the superior harmony binding together their constituent parts red it is much warmer here than in the South, Marie-Jo darling, much warmer even than when I arrived, kisses, I've taken off all my pullovers. For my book, the Australian part, I'm going to combine the letters I write to you with the labels of the 35 bark paintings sold by the department of Aboriginal Affairs, with small ads, the ones for wedding anniversaries: the children, or the couple themselves if the children are too young, announce the anniversary, there's a whole range going from wood after five years to grey sapphire after 65 (will we get that far?) with in between silver (25), pearl (30), coral (35), ruby (40), sapphire (45), gold (50), diamond (60); I'll go through the papers to see if I can find other varieties, they must exist and it's easy to invent them, I suggest brick (10), stone (15), copper (20), Platinum (55), opal (65), carbuncle (70), after 75 there would have to be the philospher's stone, elixir of life, potable gold, and you could also have plastic (1), straw (2), bark (3), paper (4); the ones for massage parlours which apparently thrive everywhere in Melbourne; the currency: the banknotes with portraits of great men (two women), as in nearly all other countries; the coins are zoological: on the reverse there is always the same queen, on the obverse, with the denomination: one cent opossum, two dragon lizards, five echidna, ten lyre-bird, 20 platypus, 50 the emu and the kangaroo on either side of the coat of arms of the six states red Minnie has painted where she lives as an orange rectangle lightened by wavy lines, where are you Irène, what are you up to, what are you thinking about at the other distant end of the unknown world, surrounded by a large black margin red the water-snake Aniautjunu came from a lagoon in the North in the dreamtime, where are you Mathilde, say the people of Oenpelli, and on arriving at Obiri found that it was a good site

PLATYPUS   (0 0)   TASMANIA   (ʊ 0)   DINGO   (0 0)   ELIXIR so he painted his image on the cliff face, then he and his family entered the fissure which opens at night to let them out to search for food. When we want to populate our ponds with more of the water-snakes we enjoy eating, we come in the right season and beat the painting affectionately, scattering his spirits red and there will also be at least a few lines missing on the Australian Cinematograph, a short story by Henry Lawson, the forbidden ballads of the penal era on the other side of the other end of the world without end, the airline companies, the tourists in the desert red the Man on the $A10 note: entertainment compiled from writings of Henry Lawson to mark the fiftieth anniversary of his death in 1922 in the subject catalogue red the third card is about home electrical appliances, dedicated to SA and the echidna, far, far away, caption: bottle tree or Australian baobab, this tree is remarkable for its bottle-shaped trunk, although it is only nine to 12 m tall, it may have a girth of 18 m, and contains 30 gallons of stored water in summer red the general name of New Holland has been given to a vast series of lands, or islands, which extends from the sixth to the 34th degree S between 105 and 140°E of Paris. It was apt to name it thus, since it was mainly Dutch navigators who explored the different parts of this country at the faraway end of the unknown world. The first land discovered in these parts was Concord Land, otherwise known as the Land of Eendracht after the name of the vessel sailed by the person who found it in 1616 between 24 and 25°S BOUGAINVILLE in 1618 another part of this land, situated around the 15th parallel, was discovered by Zeachen who gave it the name Arnhem and Van Diemen; and this land is not the same as that subsequently named after Diemen by Tasman. In 1619, Jan van Edels gave his name to a southern part of New Holland. Another part, situated between the 30th and 33rd parallels received the name of Leeuwin. Peter van Nuitz imposed his in 1627 on a coast which appears to be the continuation of the Leeuwin coast in the West

VERTICORDIA   (o o)   CUP   (o o)   LYRE-BIRD   (o o)   NORTHERN TERRITORY red waiting for the mails can sometimes mean something very different in England and in Australia, especially in NSW at the other end of the world. Her Majesty's Mails have been awaited with the greatest attention by bands of brigands who for many years have regularly robbed travellers and mail alike, and who continue to do so with perfect impunity because the police are quite incapable of arresting them and even of preventing them from continuing their extortions red the people of Queanbeyan tell how the police deemed it necessary to open McCarthy's grave and recover in particular a blanket belonging to the farmer on the other side of the other end of the world, and how at two o'clock in the afternoon of a fine day, just as they were beginning to dig, a cloud of darkness suddenly enveloped them red in the Recherche Gallery, named after the French vessel which explored the south coast in 1792 with the Espérance under the command of Bruny d'Entrecasteaux, naming several points between Leeuwin and the gulf, a display deals with the museum building itself, on the other side of the other end of the world without end, built by convicts as a lunatic asylum red we dragged the ship a little higher COOK to repair its leak red the people of Groote Eylandt believe that in the dreamtime a group of star-people accompanied by their children caught a large non-venomous snake which they cooked and ate, that then their eyes became so bright that even people on Earth can see them, far, far away, that they are the stars of the Southern Cross, and that the star-man Tjirupun lives with his numerous wives and children in a round hut of stellar grass, and that the Walagugu star-people camp by the light of the Earth above red back home at The Antipodes: Australian Folklore, a dictionary of lore, legends and popular allusions; Australia, Australia, the Pioneer years at the end of the world; Every Bird of Australia Illustrated; The Flinders Ranges red by dialling a number in Sydney at the other end of the world, you can hear the latest news red on the back of a bark painting

PLASTIC   (0 0)   NUYTSIA   (0 0)   SOUTHERN CROSS   (0 0)   KANGAROO journey to Seagull Island on the other side of the other end of the world: in one corner three dolphins which the men have tried unsuccessfully to spear: the cross-hatched rectangles indicate the rough water they had to cross, the white dots by the side of the canoe are the eggs. On the left of the other panel frightened seagulls fly off, on the right they are sitting quietly on their nests, in the centre two fish which the parents have brought back for their young red since the '67 referendum organized mainly by the Federal Council for the Advancement of Aboriginals and Torres Strait Islanders, you can read in the Opal Centre on the other unknown side of the other end of the vast world without end, there has been a trend towards a more popularly based association and a feeling that the admission of one or two Black Australians to the upper reaches of white society is not enough red this region as a whole bears a significant name on old maps: "reserve for the Blacks". It is here that the Natives have been brutally driven by the colonists. Far away. They have been left, on distant plains, in inaccessible woods, a few well-defined places where the Aboriginal race will gradually die out VERNE any white man, whether colonist, immigrant, squatter or bushman, can cross into these reserves. Only the Black must never leave red it was in 1918 that the late Ernie Sherman bought three of the most beautiful stones ever extracted: the Empress, the Pride of Australia, far, far away, and the Black Prince, a total weight of 500 carats, for the then exorbitant price of 2,000 pounds red it is thought that Polynesians from the Marquesas arrived at Easter Island around 500 AD, on the wall of my room in college; they were very religious and built many altars, invented hieroglyphs at the end of the world, and the abundance of volcanic rocks allowed them to develop megalithic sculpture whose final flowering was a series of immense human figures sometimes more than 12 m tall. Even before the arrival of the first Europeans intertribal wars had begun to destroy their society

VICTORIA   (0 0)   EURO   (0 0)   STRAW   (0 0)   CALYTHRIX diseases of the old world and the new hastened their end red hostie = air hostess at the other end of the world; oldie = old-time song red when one of us dies, after he has danced all night on the Isle of Dambalia with his hands full of red yam flowers, say the people of Yirrkala on the other side of the other end of the vast unknown world, in the morning he and the boatman set out towards where Venus rises for the distant Isle of Purelko. They travel for many days accompanied by dolphins. A masked plover announces their arrival, and the chief of the dead, Jaualinwura with the painted penis, comes to welcome them red G. C. Mundy in Our Antipodes (1855) describes the bunyip as half-horse half-alligator on the other side of the other end of the world without end, haunting the large marshes and the lagoons of the interior red what are the art-forms of the Aborigines? To depict incidents from their hunting and love life, the activities of their great ancestors, and the inhabitants of the sea and sky, they use for pigments red, brown and yellow ochres, white clay and black of charcoal, which they mix with liquid fat or orchid juice, and for brushes, twigs, feathers or their fingers red Toby Ginger and his family can rent or buy their house, and if they want to move they can take it with them, far, far away; each house is worth around $A6,400, and funds are advanced by the Department of the Interior and the Office of Aboriginal Affairs red clean, fun-loving guy, 35 separated, seeks attractive females to 35 for friendship and outings, photo if possible; kisses; continental couple, 40 and 45, would like to meet attractive woman same age or younger for dining out, theatre outings and fun times; Christians without Partners meet Thursday 15 July 7.30 p.m. St Paul's Presbyterian Church; charming lady 39, unattached, very attractive, slim, would like to meet mature man any nationality interested in dancing, theatre, yoga red at the Polynesian Village on Daydream Island the pool is the centre of attraction

SWORDFISH   (O O)   EMU   (O O)   WALLAROO   (O O)   BARK have a swim, relax on the lawns surrounding it or enjoy a drink at the bar in the middle—a perfect place to daydream red *Islands in the Sun* (0 0) LETTERS FROM THE ANTIPODES (0 0) *bird calls* on the sleeve of a record from a few years back: morning chorus, with blue wren, grey-cheeked thrush and rufous whistler; laughing kookaburra, usually live in pairs or family parties and are found mainly on the east and south coasts; call like a human laugh as they croak, cackle and suddenly explode into great peals, heard mostly at Sunrise and Sunset; "superb" lyre-bird, inhabits the dense undergrowth of forests in the SE from South QLD to VIC, male renowned for his magnificent tail feathers which he unfolds in the shape of a lyre, sets up a number of stages where he can dance or sing his love songs in the middle of winter, a wonderful virtuoso imitating nearly all the birds around, on this recording the satin bower bird, currawong, thrush, rosella, kookaburra, black cockatoo, golden widgeon, red wattle bird and raven red Great Keppel Island—great beach, great fishing, great cruises to coral reefs, great island walks, kisses, a great way to relax or get a suntan—a great fun-time is waiting for you red if this scheme to move from his hut to a house works for Toby Ginger,—what can you hear, Cécile, what are you reading, what are you doing far away?—it will help break the chain red discreet adventurous Rockhampton QLD couple wish to meet anyone, including tourists, seeking variety, new experiences and freedom from inhibitions; what can you hear Agnès, what are you looking at, where are you? divorced, sincere, depressed gent 33, wishes to meet lady 25–35 in same situation for outings, friendship view new life far, far way; wanderers invite widows, divorcees and unattached females to tonight's meeting, dancing, refreshments, supper, terrific music; male or female homosexuals ring for information red the paper Once a Week of 31 December 1865 states that the Bulla Bulla bunyip is bigger than an elephant

MACROZAMIA   (0 0)   ERIDANUS   (0 0)   OPOSSUM   (0 0)   SOUTH resembles a bullock, has eyes like glowing coals, what can you hear Irène, what are you dreaming about, what are you eating at the end of the vast unknown world, and tusks like a walrus red how do Aborigines paint on bark? In Eastern Arnhem Land they cover the entire surface with paintings of animals and totemic plants, of ancestors who are often snakes, also of clouds, rain, waves or other aspects of the land- or seascape at the other end of the world. In the West they depict totemic animals and mythical creatures, mostly X-ray figures on a plain background. On Groote Eylandt totemic animals, the lives of ancestors and sky-world mythology appear on a black, yellow or red background red postie = postman on the other side of the other end of the world; goodie = windfall red when one of us dies and arrives at the Isle of Purelko, say the people of Yirrkala on the other side of the other end of the world without end, if he is old, the chief with the painted penis rejuvenates him, if he is sick he cures him, if he is evil he makes him good, then offers him food and wives red today the three famous opals far away would be priceless red atomic blast at Mururoa further round the map: France, a non-signatory to the '63 treaty banning atmospheric tests, began its own in '66 red '70 saw the first attempt at setting up an entirely black popularly-based organization, you can read at the Opal Centre at the end of the world, the National Tribal Council, and a month later the first press conference of Black Australians and the protest against the bicentenary red as he rode along, Paganel discussed the grave question of indigenous races. There was only one opinion possible in this respect, that the British system was causing the destruction of conquered tribes and their disappearance from the lands of their ancestors at the other end of the world. This fatal tendency was in evidence everywhere, and in Australia more than elsewhere VERNE in the colony's early days, the deportees, the colonists themselves, regarded the Blacks as wild animals. They hunted them down and shot them

PADEMELON   (O O)   PAPER   (O O)   MELALEUCA   (O O)   FURNACE massacred them, invoking the authority of legal experts to prove that as the Australian was outside the domain of natural law, the murder of these wretches did not constitute a crime. The Sydney papers even proposed an effective means of disposing of the Lake Hunter tribes: by poisoning them en masse red by dialling a number in Sydney on the other side of the other end of the world, you can hear the sporting results red crucifixion and resurrection on the back of a bark painting: because of the Christian theme all the figures are dressed: Christ who is bigger than the thieves is in shorts with vertical stripes, the soldiers with heavy spears have RAAF uniforms; there were airforce bases in Arnhem Land during the second world war. The Nativity on the back of another: beneath the bark roof in the centre, Mary is seated holding the child, with Joseph beside her. Alongside, a conical mat for covering the baby, a couple of dogs, two hunting bags hanging from forked sticks; the star above; through the bush come hunters with presents of weapons or game for the child, one with a wallaby over his shoulder; a woman brings two game bags; spears, woomeras, an axe red the people of Milingimbi believe that in the dreamtime the Moon-man Alinda who lived at the mouth of the river had two wives who had each given him a son. One day, while they were out looking for food, he sent his sons to catch fish while he remained at the camp to finish making a large string bag. Far away. The children did not catch any fish, but they caught a whistling duck in a lagoon; instead of bringing it back to their father, they cooked and ate it on the spot, saying on their return that they had found nothing, but the shrewd old Moon-man noticed the fat on their hands; when they were asleep, he carefully put them into his bag. Finding themselves imprisoned, they cried and struggled, then confessed their misdeed, promising that if they were freed they would always bring back any food they laid their hands on

ECHIDNA   (0 0)   WESTERN   (0 0)   CURRAWONG   (0 0)   WOOD but Alinda would have none of this, closed the end, put the bag on his shoulder, loaded it into his canoe, and drowned them far out at sea. Meanwhile his wives were digging up yams in the jungle. When they returned they saw the Moon-man sitting in his straw hut, but no sign of the children. To their questions he replied gruffly that they had gone hunting and would not be back that evening. The worried wives waited until he was asleep, and by following the tracks they discovered what had happened; in their fury they set fire to Alinda's hut, rejoicing as they saw him die in the flames, but under their very eyes the charred body of the Moon-man came back to life, changed into a thin crescent which became a great silvery sphere and climbed to the top of a tree from where he spoke as follows to the fish, birds, other animals and men: I have decided that as from today, everybody shall die and shall never live again, save myself, for with the exception of three days each month I shall live forever red back home at The Antipodes: bird song record red in the Sultan Gallery, named after the English steamship which was the first vessel to enter the new harbour at the mouth of the Swan River, in 1897, arms and armour at the end of the world, uniforms of early volunteer regiments red early this morning I sent a party of men into the country under the direction of Mr Gore to seek for refreshments at the other end of the world COOK they returned about noon with a few palm cabbages and one or two bunches of wild bananas, far smaller than any I had ever seen, but with an excellent flavour red corroboree or native dance: the Aborigines, uncivilized though they may be, still enjoy themselves after their own fashion. The males form a semicircle with spears in their hands, making a piercing savage chant while simultaneously contorting their bodies into grotesque postures. The females beat out time on the opossum rugs they use as drums. Doubtless for them it's a delightful music red the people of Queanbeyan go on to tell how when they began to uncover the grave of the shepherd McCarthy, just as a trooper's spade struck a log that covered the body of the murdered man, a terrible explosion shook the air

LESCHENAULTIA   (0 0)   CRANE   (0 0)   MIMI   (0 0)   DRAGON LIZARD and reverberated among the surrounding hills on the other side of the other end of the world without end. The earth trembled and seemed to sink beneath the feet of the men present as if it had been struck by a huge thunderbolt red the fourth card is about means of communication far away, dedicated to NSW and the lyre-bird; caption: Coolangatta QLD, Tweed Heads NSW Captain Cook Memorial and Lighthouse, the first in the world to use a helium neon laser tube, situated at Point Danger on the border red in the same year 1628 between the tenth and the 20th parallels, far, far away, the great Gulf of Carpentaria BOUGAINVILLE was discovered by the Dutchman Peter Carpenter, whose nation has subsequently often explored the whole of its coastline red there will also be at least a few lines missing on the painted glass in the Sydney pubs, Lovecraft's Australia, fire, noises in the desert red the World of the Living Dead, preface by Lawson, in the author and title catalogue; the Auld Shop and the New, written especially for "the chief" George Robertson of Angus & Robertson, as some small acknowledgment of his splendid generosity during years of trouble and addressed to Donald Angus at the other end of the dazzling unknown world by H. Lawson; red Siglinda Ink has painted where he lives in three broad strips: orange for the sky, red for the horizon, dark yellow for the foreground, with the whole surrounded by a black margin as if it were a funeral notice, with an enormous black signature red in the dreamtime there lived in the rocky country, say the people of Oenpelli, the man Biwit who was expert at killing crocodiles; one day, after he had made a great slaughter, he transformed himself into a nameless creature which haunts the lagoon at the base of the plateau red their texture, which ranges from the most supple to the very taut, matches so perfectly the limited yet extremely rich range of colours on which they draw, that the immediate pleasure one obtains from them tends to be confused with that imparted by the shells from the same region—cones, kisses, volutes and others—which are all fascinating BRETON they seem to borrow from them the full sweep of their patterns: even the underlying glow of mother-of-pearl is not lacking red I would like

NEW SOUTH WALES   (0 0)   BANDICOOT   (0 0)   BRICK   (0 0)   BORONIA each part of this book, Marie-Jo darling, to be visually quite distinct from the others, so that when one looks at a page one gets an immediate feeling of the region concerned. So the Jungle pages will be rectangles with no blanks; in the Ceremony I Missed they will be divided horizontally into two: above will be my trip to Vancouver Island, below will be your trip with extracts from the Cold at Zuni; the southern hemisphere regions will have running titles at the bottom of the page; Archipelago with its very short paragraphs will have its running title in the centre, and its text in the four corners. All of this is still very far from being settled *free hand* (o o) LETTERS FROM THE ANTIPODES (o o) *memorial to Raymond Roussel* if you go to Toowoomba on the watershed at the edge of the Darling Downs, do not fail to visit its premier tourist attraction, acclaimed world-wide, featured by press, radio, television, the only wholly rotating camera obscura in the world, near the waterfall at Picnic Point red I also want to bring in spelling variants, which'll cause an outcry, Marie-Jo darling, to characterize each region by the repetition of a letter: for Bicentenary Kit it will be the b because of the repetition of the word "blue", for Carnival i and j (so that there are lots of dots around above each line, like masks), and for Letters from the Antipodes, kisses, o because very many Aboriginal words that have been retained contain an oo, so much so that it becomes their sigla, the watch the outback keeps on the European world surrounding it (thus one of the smartest Sydney suburbs is called Woolloomooloo); now the double o, which is very rare in French (zoo, coopération . . .) is on the contrary very commonly found in basic English vocabulary and is characteristic of Saxon words before the Norman Conquest (book = livre, cook = cuisinier, cool = frais, doom = malédiction, door = porte etc.), and lastly the double o in English hotels, and in French hotels through imitation, designates the latrines; the name of Waterloo, which is an extremely proud one on the other side of the Channel

.

CLOCK   (o o)   MANGUNMAL   (o o)   PLATYPUS   (o o)   QUEENSLAND has led wits to call the "waterclosets" of London the "loos" (a few years ago there was a delightful Guide to the London Loos) and Australian wits call Woolloomooloo the loo. This repetition of letters has an additional Australian characteristic: for small ads are as a rule ordered alphabetically within each section, which has led those who want to come first to start their text with the letter a and even to multiply the initial a's: "AAAttractive young waitresses . . .". Each section could also be characterized by one of the colours of the Zuni societies used in the Shalako and used again for the masks in Bicentenary Kit. Thus LA would be red, BK would obviously be blue, with a tinge of turquoise, stained by the green dollar, CM as white as snow, J black, Archipelago yellow, Carnival rainbow-coloured. And the same for an art-form: LA: bark paintings, BK: blues, C: floats, A: prints, and J animal calls red satin bower bird, builds bowers or arbours, lives in pairs in the East during the mating season, gathers in flocks in autumn and winter, voice a curious mixture of rasping sounds and imitations of birds around, builds an entrance of twigs. What are you dreaming about Mathilde, what are you eating, what are you looking at? Spur-winged plover, found in fields and marshes, strong, piercing warning-cry, aggressive at breeding-time, gives its cry if disturbed and swoops down on the intruder, then flies up and swoops again, makes its nest in a hole in the ground or a tuft of grass. Grey thrush, habitat dense forest, humid regions, deserts, renowned for the beauty of its clear, full notes, one of the stars of our feathered opera, especially in spring and summer red in the dreamtime Mistress Adurimja spent her time collecting and cooking water-lily bulbs for her large family; now they all live at the bottom of a water hole, what are you looking at, Cécile, what are you dreaming about, say the people of Oenpelli, and the mopokes, night birds, were quiet people who only ate cabbage-palm leaves and decorated their heads with feathers red moreover Australia has a poetic magnetism. What are you looking at Agnès, what are you thinking about far away? The curiosity of children has long been regaled by the uniqueness of its mammalian fauna—marsupials and monotremes—which seems expressly created to sanction the idea

KOALA   (0 0)   STONE   (0 0)   ISOPOGON   (0 0)   SEA SERPENT or the illusion of a lost world red on the front of the reddish-orange and black $A20 note, next to stylized propellers in full flight, Kingsford-Smith. EB: Sir Charles Edward (1897–1935), Australian aviator born at Hamilton, Brisbane, 9 February. In '27 flew round the Australian continent in ten days. The following year flew from Oakland, California to Brisbane. Most celebrated flight the crossing of the Atlantic from Port Marnock, Ireland to Harbour Grace, Canada 23–25 June '30. Was lost near Singapore while on a flight starting from London on 6 November '35 which was to end in Australia red I don't know the name of the child who has painted where he lives as an enormous black wave in front of a yellow horizon at the end of the world, with the red ochre Sun with its red and black ochre rays setting against the white sky and the occasional brown cloud red the Englishman Dampier had set out from Great Timor Isle and in 1687 at the other end of the world had made his first voyage along the coast of New Holland BOUGAINVILLE landing between Arnhem and Van Diemen Land; this very short journey had yielded no discovery. In 1699 he set out from England with the express intention of exploring the whole of these parts about which the Dutch were not making public the knowledge they possessed. He covered the west coast from the 28th to the 15th parallel. He sighted Concord Land, de Witt Land, and surmised that there could exist a passage to the South of Carpentaria. He then returned to Timor whence he returned to visit the Isles of Papua, skirted New Guinea, discovered the passage which bears his name, gave the name New Britain to the large island which forms this strait to the East, and took up course for Timor by way of New Guinea. It was the same Dampier who, from 1683 to 1691, now a pirate, now a trader, had gone round the world by changing ship red there will also be at least a few lines missing on wine labels, Apollinaire's Australian in the Murdered Poet on the other side of the other end of the world, the architecture of Brisbane and the salt lakes of the desert red the people of Queanbeyan go on to tell how when the thunder had died away

LYRE-BIRD   (O O)   TASMANIA   (O O)   BARRAMUNDI   (O O)   COPPER as the shepherd McCarthy's grave was opened, there was a roaring in the hills, and in the half light a large bull of immaculate whiteness came rushing down on the other side of the other end of the red unknown world without end. The frightened police officers sought shelter and drew their revolvers, but the animal headed for the grave where it stopped and looked around while it pawed the ground, then began moaning, lay down and died. The men went up one by one to establish that it was well and truly dead, then they resumed the exhum- ation and set up camp more than a mile away red the fifth card is about laundry, and is dedicated to TAS and the platypus: egg-laying mammal about 61 cm long, with a furry coat, a rubbery bill like that of a duck, webbed feet and a broad flat tail like that of a beaver, habitat TAS and the Eastern continent in rivers and freshwater lakes, lives in a nest at the end of a long burrow made in river banks where the female lays two or three soft-shelled eggs which hatch in 2 weeks, feeds mainly on worms, tadpoles, small prawns and aquatic insects red this morning four natives came down to the sandy point, one old and the rest young. Their features were not unpleasant, their voices soft and melodious and they were able to repeat many words after us COOK but neither we nor Tupia could understand a single one of theirs red Aboriginal sepulchre: great mourning follows death in a tribe, with men cutting themselves and women shaving their hair and covering their heads with moistened white clay at the end of the world. Sometimes the corpse is doubled up or burnt, but usually it is placed on sticks at the water's edge as in this picture, and it is believed that after death you are resurrected as a White red back home at The Antipodes: TAA Holidays, Islands in the Sun and the Great Barrier Reef at the other end of the world; Sydney Highlights red in the Shepherd Room, named after the first English ship to leave Fremantle in 1840 with a full load of WA products, the history of transport on the Swan River red

CROTALARIA   (0 0)   HYDRUS   (0 0)   BUMABUMA   (0 0)   KANGAROO the Wawalag sisters on the back of a bark painting: on their way from the South they camped by a sacred waterhole in the depths of which the great python Julunggul rests. When the elder sister gave birth to a baby, Julunggul smelt the blood of the afterbirth, came out and swallowed both sisters and the child. He is shown curled up in his lair, surrounded by his companions the caterpillars, and a cabbage-palm red the people of Milingimbi believe that in the dreamtime the old opossum Kapali, his wives, two crows, and their brother Inua lived on the coast South of Elcho Island; having quarrelled with them, he left them and their brothers behind and set out for the island in a canoe. The three crows set up a net at the mouth of a nearby river, from which they brought back every morning baskets full of fish which they cooked and ate, littering the ground around them with fishbones. Far away. When the old man returned tired from his long journey, he asked his wives for something to eat, but they harshly replied that he'd just have to find his own food; disheartened, he warmed himself by the fire and retired to sleep. On seeing this his wives got hold of burning embers and threw them over him. The old man jumped screaming into the sea to ease the pain while his wives hid in the jungle. Inua was at the nets when he heard the commotion. Suspecting something was up, he ran to the camp, put the fish-bones together to make a long ladder, and climbed up into the sky, pulling it up behind him. When his wounds had healed a little, the old opossum went to see his relatives the fish and told them of the treatment he had received from the crows. The mullet, the barramundi and the catfish were so angry over the ill-treatment of their cousin that they organized an expedition, surrounded the women's camp, speared them, and buried them in the jungle. The next day, when the crow people called in, they couldn't find the wives, and, examining the ground reconstituted what had happened

NORTHERN TERRITORY   (0 0)   WOMBAT   (0 0)   SILVER   (0 0)   REGELIA when he first heard of this Inua refused to believe that Kapali had exacted such a vengeance when a good beating would in his opinion have been quite sufficient, but when the crows told him what they had seen: the broken spears, the ground spattered with blood, the corpses, he had to yield to the facts. Climbing down to Earth on his fishbone ladder, he brought his sisters to life, took them up into the sky with him, and changed them into stars. Ever since the three of them have lived happily on the banks of the Milky Way, safe from the revenge of the old opossum whose fury has not yet abated red it is clear that in the early days of their conquest the English had recourse to murder in the cause of colonization. Their cruelty was atrocious. They behaved in Australia as they did in India, where 500,000 Indians died; or as in Cape Province, where a population of 1,000,000 Hottentots had fallen to 100,000 VERNE thus the Aboriginal population, decimated by ill-treatment and drink, is in the process of disappearing from the continent in the face of a homicidal culture. Certain governors, it is true, issued edicts aimed at the bloodthirsty bushmen! They punished with a few strokes of the whip the White who cut off a Black's nose and ears, or removed his little finger "to make a pipe-cleaner". Empty threats! The murders were organized on a vast scale and whole tribes disappeared. Just to take the case of Van Diemen Island, it had 5,000 natives at the beginning of the century, but by 1863 the number of inhabitants had been reduced to seven! And very recently the Mercury could actually report the arrival at Hobart Town of the last of the Tasmanians red by dialling a number in Sydney at the end of the world, you can hear the mining company prices red 38 of the 43 known species of birds of paradise live in New Guinea on the wall of my room red since 1970 black organizations have spread throughout the country, you can read at the Opal Centre on the other side, our people are no longer prepared to be confined to camps on the outskirts of country towns, clothed in rags on the fringe of White society

INDIAN　　　(0 0)　　　BAMUNIT　　　(0 0)　　　EMU　　　(0 0)　　　VICTORIA

so the Black Australians are becoming more active than ever red when one of us dies and he has met his new wives and satisfied his hunger, say the people of Yirrkala, other world, he meets his old friends again. At Purelko there is neither want, nor quarrels, nor misfortune. Food abounds, the swamps and sea are full of fish, the forests full of emus and kangaroos, and it is never cold red in 1930 fine opals were discovered about 190 miles SE of Coober Pedy, far away, the latest of the great opal rushes was underway red where can Aboriginal rock engravings be found? Practically throughout Australia. Far, far away. The simplest are short, narrow grooves arranged haphazardly, the finest occur on large expanses of sandstone in the East of NSW where figures of animals, humans, ancestors, weapons and implements may be seen, often in fine, life-sized compositions (one whale is 20 m long), the most secret, found in the interior, are hammered all over their surface with small animals, their tracks, humans, geometric designs red Elsie = queen of England at the end of the red unknown world; Sammie = president of the United States red seeking good-looking plumpish lady, age no concern, lacking love and companionship, am new to Brisbane, 40, average height, easy going, send photo; at the other end Metropolitan Church, homos, God loves you too, every Sunday at 7.30 p.m. red E. Lloyd in his Visit to the Antipodes with some Reminiscences of a Sojourn in Australia (1846) writes that the head of the bunyip is like that of an emu with a long beak at the extremity of which there is a transverse projection on either side with serrated edges like the bone of the sting-ray on the other side. Its body and legs are those of an alligator. Its hind legs are remarkably thick and strong, the fore legs much longer. The extremities have long claws, but the Aborigines state that it usually kills by hugging red the Great Barrier Reef surrounds you on the coral platform of Heron Island where spectacular coral growths and tropical fish of unbelievable shapes and colours will keep you fascinated for days, kisses

GOANNA (0 0) PEARL (0 0) BEAUFORTIA (0 0) HARE

delights are in store for you on Heron Island red how are you getting on Toby Ginger red *health problems* (0 0) LETTERS FROM THE ANTIPODES (0 0) *talk* recorded in English for the ABC in '68 when I was invited through the cultural services of the French Embassy to take part in writer's week at the Adelaide Festival, I came in the first place because the whole trip was a kind of challenge, a game. The idea of going all those kilometres for just one week had something very exciting about it. I wanted to experience a new kind of fatigue: the change of time, the giddiness, the intoxication of feeling all those countries, all those seas gliding silently beneath my uncomfortable sleep. I travelled via the United States, with a week of lectures on my way out, and one on the way back. There was also the added spice of crossing the international date line for the first time red of course these poor, sick, twilight people have not done this all on their own. Of course kind, tormented, pallid people have come and worked with them. Kisses. How are you getting on now Toby Ginger red when the bunyip is in the water it swims like a frog, writes the author of a Visit to the Antipodes, when it is on shore it gets up on its hind legs, with its head held nearly four metres high. What are you doing Irène, where are you at the other end? Its breast is said to be covered with different coloured feathers, but it is likely that the Blacks have never been able to get close enough to ascertain whether this appearance might not arise from scales or hair red Tangalooma, for people of action, on Moreton Island for waterskiing, landrover safaris, fishing, aquaplaning, squash, tennis or just relaxing by the pool. What are you doing Mathilde, on the other side? Tangalooma where time disappears on Moreton Island red tellie = television; what are you doing Cécile, what are you eating on the other side of the other inverted end of the unknown world without end? movie = cinema red

MIKMIK   (0 0)   OPOSSUM   (0 0)   SOUTH   (0 0)   DUGONG

Rockhampton working man seeks slim brunette for paid daytime meetings; refined couple wish to meet ladies fed up with not getting the most out of life
red the various opal rushes have taken place on the edge of a former sea, far,
far away, which has been dried up for millions of years red what are Aboriginal
cave paintings like? The series reproduced in the exhibition includes a fish, lizard,
kangaroo, man, turtle, woman, serpent, tracks, Wandjina heads, stencilled hands
and boomerangs, concentric circles, a fine totemic figure of three circles and
finally the striking group of the lightning brothers Yagtjadbulla and Tcabuinji
with his wife under his arm, the ancestors of the lightning totem closely associated with the rain totem and rainmaking ceremonies of the Vardaman people
of the NT, three and four metres tall in the Delamere cave red the Aboriginal
Embassy was set up in front of the federal parliament on 26 January '72, you
can read at the Opal Centre at the other end, in order to protest against the
fact that the Black Australians are the only indigenous people in the world without the right to reserve land, to whom no form of compensation has ever been
offered, and also to demand statehood for the NT so that they can have their
small say in federal government with members of the House of Representatives
and the six senators to whom the NT would be entitled. Also the establishment
of a parliament with the constitutional right to negotiate with foreign undertak-
ings, float overseas loans, have responsibility for education and infantile mortality red when one of us dies and arrives at Purelko, say the people of Yirrkala
on the other unknown side of the other end of the inverted world, he has not
finished his trials. One day, as he is walking among the trees, he surprises two
women who take fright and run to warn their menfolk of the presence of a
stranger. They form themselves into a line, spear in hand, and wait for him.
Seeing this, he attempts to distract their attention by dancing; but when he
has finished the spirit-men of Purelko spear him one after the other. The first
spears penetrate deeply, but with each thrust his body hardens and the last
ones can no longer scratch him. Meanwhile the spirit-women sitting on the
ground weep in sympathy for his sufferings

CORAL   (0 0)   CALOTHAMNOS   (0 0)   WOLF   (0 0)   ECHIDNA when the ordeal is over the spirit-men lead their new brother into their camp, teach him new songs, new dances, and have him join in their sacred ceremonies red by dialling a number in Sydney, other world, you can hear the petroleum company prices red Cook's voyage in the Endeavour from 1768–71 set the precedent for taking naturalists and artists on voyages of exploration, on the wall of my room in college. As a result, the British Admiralty organized the voyage of the Beagle in 1831–36 with Darwin and the painters Augustus Earle and Conrad Martens. Banks's herbarium remains an irreplaceable source of information on the Pacific red the people of Milingimbi believe that our Orion, Hyades and Pleiades constellations along with others far, far away form a large canoe in which the star-men paddle along the Milky Way river red Blacks hunted by the Whites like game, with all the refined emotions engendered by this kind of sport; fires spread far and wide so that the inhabitants should be no more spared than the bark "gunyahs" they use as dwellings, in Mistress Branican. The conquerors have even gone as far as to use mass strychnine poisoning at the end of the world, which permitted a more rapid destruction VERNE and the following words, from the pen of an Australian colonist, have been recorded: whenever I encounter men on my land, I shoot them, because they are cattle killers; the women too, because they give birth to cattle killers; the children as well, because they would become cattle killers red in the Calista Room, named after an English vessel, the first to bring people to settle the Swan River colony in 1829, relics from the age of sail, photographs of sailors and ships in the harbour of bygone days at the other unknown end of the inverted world, models of clippers, an enormous wheel red the great hunter on the back of a bark painting: standing by a sacred waterhole formed by the Glyde River; abundant wildlife all around

WESTERN   (O O)   TURTLE   (O O)   RUBY   (O O)   WARATAH on the right, the fish he catches, on the left, insects, bees and birds, in the centre, lizard, kangaroo, emu, snake. On the other side. The funeral rites of the Manarrngu re-enact his life and death red Christmas on the diggings or the unwelcome visitor: in the Antipodes it is usually the hottest time of the year. The new arrivals, with their minds filled with all the associations from the old country, feel ill at ease when instead of frost they encounter a shade temperature of 95° and poisonous snakes who seek your hospitality with perfect nonchalance, especially in the bush red the sixth card is about my books, far away, dedicated to VIC and to the kangaroo emu couple; caption: Numinbah Valley QLD, the natural arch from inside the cave red they must wear from time to time a kind of fillet on their head at the unknown end of the inverted world COOK for one of them used for this purpose a piece of an old shirt I had given them red and there will also be at least a few lines missing on butterflies, especially the Papilio Ulysses which is captured by placing a preserved female on the ground, the idea mentioned in one of the first poems published in Australia that God had first created the world in four parts and said that he was well pleased, and that it was only afterwards that the last part crept in with its blasphemous and parodic continent at the other end, culinary possibilities and the clouds lost in the desert red the people of Queanbeyan go on to tell how four days after the apparition of the white bull, one of the police officers returned to the grave with the farmer, intending to bury some poisoned flour nearby. The animal had gone. On the other side. Waterloo Tom was condemned to death, reprieved, and spent the rest of his days in prison red nor· do I know the name of the child who has painted where he lives with orange earth, a red horizon with a big black blob, other world, and a dark orange sky with low brown clouds and two black trees red since our return to France English navigators have come back from another journey round the world. The name of the ship is the Endeavour

TABLE MOUNTAIN   (0 0)   MUNIMUNIGAN   (0 0)   DRAGON LIZARD   (0 0)   SOUTH WALES it was under the command of Captain Cook and had as passengers Banks and Solander, two famous scientists BOUGAINVILLE the account of the sea voyage has already appeared red the knowledge that it harbours in its northern part quite homogeneous human communities whose "clock" is several millenia behind ours is calculated to incite us to go and see for ourselves BRETON but it is quite a different matter to see, far away, and subsequently to grasp the very substance of what one has seen: then you have Gauguin's "I'm off to the Marquesas. At last!" red DAB: went to Canada with his family at the age of six, his father having been appointed superintendent on the Canadian Pacific Railway at the end of the world. During the voyage the youngest son was discovered hanging from a hawse-hole on the side of the ship, showing a friend how to join him. Almost drowned off Sydney's Bondi Beach a few years later, and given up for dead, but a nurse succeded in bringing him back to life after hours of effort. At the outbreak of the '14 war obtained his parents' permission to enlist on his 18th birthday, 9 February 1915. Trained as a dispatch rider, served in Egypt, Gallipoli and France. In October '16 was one of 140 men chosen from the ranks of the AIF to train in England as an aviator. Saw action in France before the end of 1917, and obtained the Military Cross for shooting down a two-seater, setting fire to some huts, and machine-gunning a column of Germans who were getting ready to attack. Wounded in the foot a few days later, and lost three toes red sulphur-crested cockatoo, found throughout the continent except in certain Western and Southern regions, favourite food standing wheat which it plunders in droves. During these sorties one or two sentinels usually remain perched on poles or trees and give the alarm at the slightest sign of danger, whereupon the entire flock flies off screeching

KOOKABURRA　　(0 0)　　SAPPHIRE　　(0 0)　　ANIGOSANTHOS　　(0 0)　　MICROSCOPE crow, found mainly in mountainous regions of the North and by rivers, feeds on carrion, insects, young birds and eggs, emits a series of short notes making a "ka-ka-ka" sound. At the other end rufous scrub bird, lives hidden in the dense undergrowth, difficult to see and record, remarkable mimic with a very powerful voice for its size, able to fly but seldom does so and then only for short distances red in the dreamtime Gumangan the crocodile and Birikbirik the plover possessed a pair of fire-sticks, say the people of Oenpelli on the other side, which were the only ones on Earth. Gumangan and Birikbirik always travelled together and it was the crocodile who did all the work because the plover was lazy. One morning as they were setting out hunting, Gumangan asked Birikbirik to light the fire, but when he returned some hours later with a large kangaroo, he found that the sleeping plover had done nothing. He berated him in fury for his laziness and ran to plunge the two sticks in the river so as to extinguish the fire for ever. But the nimble Birikbirik managed to wrest them from him just in time, thus saving fire for us red the Toowoomba camera obscura consists of a small octagonal cabin crowned by a pyramid-shaped roof ending in a sort of chimney within which a mirror projects the image it receives onto the middle of the floor. You go in through a door let into one of the eight side panels and sit on a bench round the edge. Kisses. As soon as the door is shut tight, a round, horizontal screen allows you to admire, but in a rotating, circular form, exactly what you would see outside red on the way back from Adelaide, I changed planes at Sydney, and a few rows further up, on the other side of the aisle, there was a couple reading a paper with a double spread in colour set out in an intriguing fashion. When I got to Brisbane airport, I found what I was looking for: on the front page there was a box with two little boys showing a map surrounded by a black Sun: free inside, Australia Unlimited supplement, coloured lift-out wall-map for students, can be kept or cut up for projects

NOULABIL   (0 0)   PLATYPUS   (0 0)   QUEENSLAND   (0 0)   BUNYIP

I took out the historical map and hung it up in my room by means of an ingenious system of suspension, but it's already beginning to tear, and the light will undoubtedly fade the colours *memorial to Raymond Roussel* (0 0) LETTERS FROM THE ANTIPODES (0 0) *appearance of the word kangaroo in French literature* Buffon's work is much earlier than Cook's voyage, but as it has been the basic treatise of natural history for our forbears, successive editors have striven to keep it in publication. The supplement to the article on jerboas was written by Mr Allemand: all of Europe knows that Messrs Banks and Solander, inspired by an almost heroic zeal for furthering our knowledge in astronomy and natural history, have undertaken a journey round the earth; when they returned to England, they exhibited two gerbos which surpass in size the largest of our hares; when they run on their hind legs, they throw our best dogs off the scent. These are among the least unusual things they have brought back with them; they have made a large collection which will provide them with enough material for a thousand plates. By order of the English admiralty, an account of their voyage is being prepared; it will reveal very interesting details about a country in the southern regions which so far we only know by name; I am speaking of New Zealand red I now enjoy the use of an old TV MS has given me. It's a genuine piece of furniture, Marie-Jo darling, with a smallish screen, and the cloth concealing the loudspeakers has been torn away, but it works very well provided you play around with the channel switch. Kisses. It has only one defect, a deformation that I can't correct myself, with the lines getting closer and closer as they go down, so that in the place of a circle on the screen, you see a flattened egg, and people look as if they have big heads and short legs, or if only their faces are shown they have large foreheads and little chins

GOLD   (0 0)   CEPHALOTUS   (0 0)   FLY   (0 0)   GADJIMUNGAINI the Olympic Games turn into very strange contests between intellectual dwarfs. Yesterday evening the Japanese gymnastic team's legs got longer when they were upside down. I also had the joy of seeing the first photos of Mars red my arrival point on the continent was Sydney, where I stayed for a day in a little hotel at King's Cross trying to sort out my biological clock; immediately I was fascinated. What can you hear Agnès, what are you looking at, where are you? It was only a first glimpse, through half-closed eyes, but I knew with certainty that something was waiting for me in this country, a sort of vigour which would be useful to me some day, an elixir which at some crucial point in time would soothe my mind. At the other end. And immediately I wanted to come back one day with a little more time. Of course the images from that first journey are blurred today. It was so short and so hectic. There was that extraordinary feeling of distance in comparison with where I live, along with the inversion of some fundamental terms of reference: the Sun in the North at midday, the fact that at night, when I thought I recognized a constellation near the pole, I had to correct myself in the knowledge that the stars couldn't be my familiar northern ones, that I would have to relearn the entire sky if I had time, if I was here for some time; but there was also the internal distance of the continent. I was only in cities and planes on this occasion, but in the way people spoke to me, walked, dressed, looked at articles in big stores, there was, even if they were unaware of it, the presence of the desert. Having lived for a year in Upper Egypt I had come under the fascination of the desert, just as I was to be later on in the American Far West, but the relationship between this land of immensity and the cities was different, it was coloured differently, like a bass in music it made everything sound differently red in the dreamtime Linmarara decided to create rain, what are you eating Irène, what can you hear, say the people of Oenpelli on the other side of the other distant end of the changing world, made a pole, covered it with his blood and drew lines on it in red and white down, then planted it in the ground and seated himself in front of it to sing

LYRE-BIRD   (0 0)   TASMANIA   (0 0)   COCKATOO   (0 0)   PLATINUM

Then the spirit of the red and white lines sank into the ground. He began the song again and the spirit of the pole itself sank into the ground and became a female kangaroo. Then he sang a second song and the female kangaroo flew off and urinated over immense areas of countryside. This was the first rain. And he ordered the rainbow serpent Ngaloit to leave his waterhole at Gudjamandi and spread across the sky. We can still sing his songs, but we must be careful not to let the poles hear them at the wrong season, otherwise the rainbow-serpent would drown the world red there is a camera obscura at Edinburgh in Scotland, what are you eating Mathilde, what are you up to, but only its mirror revolves, other world, not the entire hut as at Toowoomba red Flying Mathilda, early days in Australian aviation in the subject catalogue, far away, and in the author and title catalogue: The Flight of the Southern Cross red Prince Albert lyre-bird, smaller than the stately variety, does not erect stages, but dances on the ground or on logs, splendid songster with great imitative gifts; whistling eagle, lives in pairs, splendid in flight, climbs very high to project its whistle, which can be heard over immense distances, feeds on small mammals, insects, birds and carcasses, far, far away; bellbird, forms large colonies in eucalypts and remains for years in the same spot, thin metallic cry; several together sound like the ringing of a bell red leaving Plymouth on 25 August 1768, they reached Terra del Fuego on 16 January '69 after putting in first at Madeira, then at Rio de Janeiro BOUGAINVILLE they stopped for five days at the Bay of Good Success and, having rounded Cape Horn at the end of the world, they set course for Tahiti. They stayed there from 13 April to 13 July and in June they observed the transit of Venus across the disc of the Sun red an intensely bright spotlight needs to be focused on the initial, almost amorphous network of lines which the artist alone will decide to use to represent wild honey for example

BUNYA   (0 0)   LEVEL   (0 0)   PITARI   (0 0)   KANGAROO the tangle of seaweed BRETON or fire red the people of Canberra tell how in 1826 a superb diamond was stolen from a certain James Cobbity in an obscure QLD village by an escaped convict who was subsequently captured but refused to give any information in spite of frequent whippings. In 1842 he passed on his secret to a groom with a map showing the hiding place red little Daniel has been to the Salt Hole and has painted it as a white blob with a cream-coloured path leading to it on the natural-coloured paper, with a circular tent nearby made of four segments: pink, brown, yellow, black red in the morning we were visited by ten or 11 Natives; those who came on board were very keen to have some of our turtle and took the liberty of dragging two of them onto the gangway to put over the side; being frustrated in their efforts, they became a little troublesome and wanted to throw overboard everything they could lay their hands on; I offered them bread which they rejected with scorn, as I believe they would have done for anything except turtle. Shortly afterwards they went ashore and immediately one of them took a handful of grass and lit it from the fire we had on shore, and before we realized what he was intent on doing he set the grass alight in a large circle round us so that in an instant everything was in flames. Immediately afterwards they went to a spot where all our nets and a good deal of our washing had been put to dry, and tried to set fire to the grass. We managed to prevent them, but the first fire spread furiously through the woods and grasslands COOK after some unintelligible conversation they returned to a point opposite the boat where they remained for some time, then set off again and set fire to the forests within a radius of two miles red there will also be at least some lines missing on the plants and in particular the orchid that becomes impregnated by attracting a male ichneumon, which behaves towards it as it does towards its female at mating time, the shirts, far, far away, Lola Montez's journey to Australia and the flies in the desert red back home at The Antipodes I'm piecing together the remains of the coloured double spread of Australia Unlimited red the seventh card is about furniture

NORTHERN TERRITORY   (0 0)   WALLABY   (0 0)   DIAMOND   (0 0)   BLACK BOY dedicated to WA and to the termites at the other end, with the caption: evening approaches red the lesser pythons on the back of a bark painting: when the python Julunggul swallowed the Wawalag sisters, the totemic pythons from other districts saw him standing erect over his waterhole, and raising themselves similarly, asked him what he had done. The dull groaning of his confession has become the sound of the bullroarer on the other side. The small lines and dots represent eucalypt flowers floating on the sacred pond red our convicts, what we do to them, what happens to them: penal gang in TAS carrying out work that used to be prescribed some years ago, namely the carrying of bundles of wooden tiles. Each person carried two weighing 28 pounds, and they usually had to march for around 30 miles a day. Other world. This inhuman labour has now been abolished red consequently one can understand the hatred which the Australians have maintained in respect of their executioners, far away VERNE in Mistress Branican red the Challenger Gallery, now closed, named after the English ship aboard which Captain Fremantle arrived in 1829 to take possession of WA; in the Success Gallery, after the English ship in which James Stirling explored the Swan River in 1827, the history of the port of Fremantle red the cold, fish-laden Peru current and the warm equatorial current meet in the Galapagos where in 1835 Darwin (portrait), noticing that the same birds or mammals had acquired subtle differences on islands close to one another but mutually inaccessible, began to develop his theory of evolution red the people of Yirrkala believe that in the dreamtime the Moon-man Nalimba and Dirima the parrot-fish were always squabbling over petty things, and that one day each picked up his club and managed to kill the other, and that then the spirit of the Moon-man said to the spirit of Dirima: you are going to become a parrot-fish who lives in the sea and when you die you can never come to life again, but I am going to become the Moon in the sky

OCTANT   (0 0)   DAUANDJA   (0 0)   EMU   (0 0)   VICTORIA and if I die like the rest of you I will only remain dead for three days and then I will come to life again, and that the nautili are the skeletons of the dead Moon at the other end, and that in the dreamtime Nalimba spent most of his time collecting a kind of yam and that his sister Balwokman the dugong who lived in the surrounding marshes collected coarse grass, and that one day she stepped in some poisonous grass that set up an intense irritation which she tried in vain to relieve by many remedies and that finally she jumped into the sea and said to Nalimba: I am going to become a dugong and remain forever in the water which soothes me, and that the Moon-man replied to her: in that case I am going to live forever in the sky, and that one day the two Gurungurun men decided to kill Balwokman and eat her, but that Nalimba whipped up a large wave to wake her and that in disgust the Gurungurun had nothing further to do except turn themselves into pandanus trees red and when it is a woman who dies, continue the people of Yirrkala on the other side, and she arrives at Purelko, Jaualinwura sends a small child to meet her, telling it to go and find its mother, rejuvenates her if necessary, cures her of all her illnesses and makes her pregnant if she is not, and after a few months she painlessly gives birth to a child of wondrous beauty who joins the others playing in the forests of the spirits red by dialling a number in Sydney on the other side of the other end of the vast changing world without end you can hear the industrial prices from A to J red what is the Aboriginal boomerang like? The genuine ones are between 30 and 74 cm long, weigh up to 350 g, are sharply curved with the ends slightly twisted in opposite directions, a flat lower surface and a convex upper surface. It is held by one end, behind the thrower's head, with the concave edge forward; after a few running paces, the arm is bought over and the boomerang released with a powerful wrist movement. It starts descending but soon rises, rotates endwise and describes a horizontal circle up to more than 100 m in diameter and as many as four smaller circles before falling to the ground in the vicinity of the thrower

DINGO   (0 0)   OPAL   (0 0)   EUCALYPTUS   (0 0)   PEACOCK is known nowhere else in the red world red in spite of the infantile mortality rate, the number of Black Australians is increasing, you can read at the Opal Centre far, far away, three times faster than the others, they are now concentrated in the rural areas of the Centre red if you like a ball our Saturday night parties are the thing, come and join other couples and singles, air-conditioned, buffet, mix with the happy crowd at the end of the world; fun times are here again, mix with fun lovers, couples and chicks, it's your night red colour film about opal mines; you will see the hardships endured by the miners at the other end. Scenes rarely seen by tourists in Australia red Fraser Island is a natural paradise and a fisherman's dream, with trips taking you past virgin beaches, freshwater lakes and rainforests on the other side of the other changing end of the vast world, or hire a jeep and plan your own safari. You'll never forget Fraser Island red softie = woman's underclothing; naughtie = sex act red the catalyst was an Englishman, John McNeil, 52, eight years in the NT, working for nothing in the hope that he would be employed by the Apatulas in their workshop. Kisses. His wife and children returned to Alice Springs. He would say: I have had a dream red the bunyip lays eggs twice as big as an emu's, say the Aborigines to the visitor to the Antipodes, coloured pale blue and no good for eating *the bunyip* (o o) LETTERS FROM THE ANTIPODES (o o) *red dream from les Indes galantes* a park, merrymaking. I take Hébé off to one side. Osman is hesitating between Bellone and l'Amour. I slip masked into the shade. Sunlight through the branches, arched trellis laden with clusters of grapes. Harp, cello, and myself giving my red mask to Émilie in the sun's rays. Osman and Valère in a patch of golden light while Hébé calls them softly. The evening's fragrance *red dream from les Indes galantes* (o o) LETTERS FROM THE ANTIPODES (o o) *concert programme* given by the Hermannsburg Aboriginal Choir on its tour commemorating the mission's 90th anniversary

GURUWULDAN   (o o)   OPOSSUM   (o o)   EURO   (o o)   CARBUNCLE national anthem, backdrop of the new Hermannsburg church at night, with all lines leading to the open door and the altar, the story of Joseph, taken from Méhul's opera red in the Life and Adventures of William Buckley (the Wild White Man), Hobart 1852, John Morgan tells how there lives in the lakes and rivers an extraordinary amphibious animal which the Aborigines call the bunyip, whose back, apparently covered in dark grey feathers, was the only part he had ever been able to see; the creature was the size of a large calf or a little bigger. Kisses. It only appears in very fine weather and in very calm water. He could never tell whether what he saw was its head or its tail, and consequently he could never estimate its size with any certainty red falsie = padded bra; dummie = dressmaker's figure red how is your dream going, John McNeil red you can hear a description of the various types of opals as you watch them being cut and polished, and you will be offered free refreshments to make your visit more pleasant and relaxing red Dunk Island blends into a tropical environment of hibiscus, frangipani and coconut palms. Secluded beaches, mountain walks, and a seascape of reefs, atolls, coral islands surrounding Dunk Island red according to the statistics given to the Senate Committee on Social Environment by the Department of the Interior in 1972, you can read at the Opal Centre at the end of the vast changing world, Black Australians form 62 per cent of the population in rural areas of the NT red very attractive refined lady 44 wishes to meet sincere executive to 53, at the other end; Women Everywhere, a group of well-meaning, unconventional women who are trying to discover and enjoy their true nature red by dialling a number in Sydney, on the other side, you can hear the industrial prices from K to Z red how do the Aborigines fight? Warfare occurs above all between clans or local groups, but camp fights are common. Vendettas are carried on for years and result in many deaths. Wars are waged for avenging an insult or a crime, for capturing women

WATTLE   (0 0)   PHOENIX   (0 0)   NALBIDJI   (0 0)   ECHIDNA not for the land or possessions of an enemy. The most serious crimes are murder, abduction, incest, rape, adultery and ritual offences. A punitive expedition will surround the camp at night, or invade it in daylight and kill a man to avenge the death of a member of its clan or group. Many quarrels are settled by duels with spears, clubs or stone knives. In battles there can be up to fifteen men killed, but combats usually stop as soon as there are one or two seriously wounded red the people of Yirrkala believe that in the dreamtime Guripun was collecting coarse grass with his young wife and that the string tying their bundle snapped scattering their harvest far and wide; in their disgust they went up into the sky and became Arcturus and another star of our Waggoner red when one of us dies they also say far, far away, if he belongs to the jiritja moiety of our tribe, once his wooden coffin has been placed in its definitive position and everyone has returned home, his soul, which has finally separated from his bones and is guided by the cries of jungle birds, makes its way to the Northern forest where it meets the Wuluwulu spirits who guide it to the chief of the dead Nalkuma red in the Investigator Gallery, named after the English vessel in which Matthew Flinders explored the south coast in 1801–2, then sailed round the continent in 1803, the history of whaling starting with the hundreds of American and other whalers who put in during the 19th century, and of pearl-fishing red waved albatross with its wing-tip pointing to the Galapagos red here we see the bandits not only taking the mail, but tying up and robbing the police

SOUTH   (0 0)   WALLAROO   (0 0)   ELIXIR   (0 0)   BANKSIA who had come to the rescue of the unfortunate travellers red one might note in passing that the Australians respect the dead. They do not bring them into contact with the earth; they wrap the bodies in foliage or bark, and place them in shallow graves with their feet pointing towards the Rising Sun, or else they bury them upright, as is the custom in certain tribes. The grave of a chief is then covered by a hut with its entrance facing East VERNE one should also add that, among the least savage natives, the following bizarre belief has been noted, namely, that the dead will be reborn in the form of a white man red on an additional card the list of books borrowed from the library, with the caption: coconut-palm-lined beach, QLD red Yurlunggur, the great didgeridoo, on the back of a bark-painting: two men from the Djinang tribe stand with hands raised. The cross-hatched design in the centre is Yurlunggur. Far, far away. One of the men points; he imitates the pose of the men who murdered the sugar-bag man in the dreamtime. At the top two others in another ritual pose, with hands on hips. The rounded shapes are the stones which ancestors placed in the area. On the left, freshwater fish red there will also be at least a few lines missing on the female singers, the life of a surfer at the end of the world, the jelly-fish, the service stations in the desert red back home at The Antipodes little Doreen has been to Santa Teresa and her picture is full of people, swirls and colours red yesterday I sent some of our people into the country to bring back greens, and one of them strayed away from the rest and met with four natives who let him go without doing him the slightest harm COOK and seeing that he was not returning to the boat by the shortest route they put him on the right track red "Alcheringa", the time of dreams, which is also the time of all metamorphoses far away BRETON these pollen-dusted strips of eucalyptus which come from it are the ones best fitted to lead us back to it red the people of Canberra go on to tell how the Aborigine who had swallowed the diamond

PAINTER　　(0 0)　　NADIDJIT　　(0 0)　　DRAGON LIZARD　　(0 0)　　WESTERN was buried in a plot of land far, far away on the site of Yarralumla House, which became the temporary home of the Queen's representative during the setting up of the federal capital red willy wagtail, very tame, often found hopping around after insects on gates or on the backs of cattle, usually sings in the Moonlight; dawn chorus, specially rufous whistler, white-backed mapgie, crows at the end of the world; whip-bird red from there they set course so as to approach New Zealand at 40°S. They landed on its east coast on the third of October, and after six months' circumnavigation at the other dazzling end of the changing world they understood fully that, instead of belonging to the southern continent as was generally supposed, New Zealand is formed by two islands with no continent in the vicinity BOUGAINVILLE they also observed that several dialects of the Tahitian language were spoken there and were all reasonably well understood by the Tahitian they had taken on board the Endeavour red inside the Toowoomba camera obscura a charming old lady describes as they appear all the things you can see outside, on the other side, and in particular her customers' cars in the parking lot, marvelling at their beauty red on the back of the $A20 note, next to symbolic representations of old planes, the portrait of Hargrave. Nothing in the EB. DAB: Lawrence (1850–1915), aviation pioneer born in England, remained there to pursue his studies while his father came to Australia, other world, arrived in Sydney in 1866, but although he had shown an aptitude for mathematics he did not enter university red and there was the discovery of Australian wine. It wasn't just that it was very good. It was the fact that, in an English-speaking country which had so many British features at that time (the face, the skin of Australian suburbs has changed enormously in the course of a few years), there should be such an awareness of the grape, a modest pride. It wasn't at all the language of an English connoisseur talking about French wines, but the conversation of a French countryman explaining the differences and the ups and downs of the local products

PADEMELON   (0 0)   PLASTIC   (0 0)   CLIANTHUS   (0 0)   SOUTHERN FISH thanks to wine, a kind of Mediterranean element, already apparent in my first glimpse of Sydney, stood out very markedly, and I felt at home, just like all the Greeks and Italians asking their cousins to come. But it was an inverted Mediterranean, a coastal ring with the desert in the middle and the water all around, a terra mediaqua, hidden dryness in the heart of the oceans. Back home in France I was waiting for an opportunity to drink a larger draught of Australian wine, and it occurred five years ago. I travelled round the continent in five weeks, with a prelude in New Zealand. This time I knew that one day Australia would certainly play an important part in one of my books. So I looked at everything with new eyes, with one question always in my mind: how can I speak and write about what I am seeing and learning, trying to collect any useful information like the satin bower bird gathering things in blue for his twig-lined house of love red in the dreamtime a father, mother and several children lived not far from Gudjamandi, the waterhole of the rainbow-serpent Ngaloit, say the people of Oenpelli far, far away, now the parents died leaving their children in the care of their friend Wiriliup who gave them so little to eat that they cried continuously, which annoyed the rainbow-serpent who came up out of his waterhole and flooded the whole countryside, whereupon Wiriliup fled and managed to escape, but the children panicked and although they climbed into trees, they were drowned; they still live at the bottom of the Gud-jamandi waterhole and Ngaloit who has adopted them finds playmates for them red differs from all the jerboas that have hitherto been described not only by its size, which approaches that of an ewe, but also by the number and disposition of its toes. Kisses. Parkinson who accompanied Mr Banks as his artist, and whose memoirs have been published, tells us that it had five toes armed with hooked nails on its front feet, and four on its hind ones; as it was a young one which was not yet fully grown, it only weighed 38 pounds; its head, neck and shoulders were extremely small in comparison with the other parts of its body

DIGNUK   (0 0)   PLATYPUS   (0 0)   SOUTH WALES   (0 0)   CURRAWONG it moved by making very big upright leaps; it kept its front legs against its chest, and they only appeared to be used for digging; its tail was thick at the base, and its diameter grew steadily smaller towards the tip; its whole body was covered in a dark mouse-grey fur, except its head and ears, which were rather like those of a hare red this morning I went into town to see the director of cultural services in QLD, an Englishman with silky white hair who insisted on introducing me over the phone to two people I had met five years previously and whom I can't remember at all, Marie-Jo darling; I'm seeing a lady on Monday and a gentleman in August. I took advantage of my trip to walk round the magnificent botanical gardens on a bend in the river which is bounded on the other side by a high rocky cliff, then had lunch in a department store cafeteria and went looking for information in another institution for Aborigines, run largely by them, a kind of counterpart of the other one, and with the curious name of the Opal Centre. Then I bought a dictionary of white Australian folklore before I took the bus back. Next week I'll send Cécile and her sisters some cards and work as hard as I can on my book, because in August we'll get around as much as we can. For the time being I'll be working on some passages about bark paintings representing constellations from the account by Charles P. Mountford of the Anglo-American expedition to Arnhem Land in 1948. In the Centre the atmosphere is extraordinarily clear. Last Saturday at Wilpena Pound it was quite impressive. The Aborigines wove innumerable legends in the sky; I want to give some idea of them *appearance of the word kangaroo in French literature* (0 0) LETTERS FROM THE ANTIPODES (0 0) *counterpoint* commentary by Trevor Jones in 1956 in the review Oceania on recordings made in Arnhem Land in 1952 by A. Elkin: the most important structural aspect of this cycle is the use of deferred imitative entries and the simultaneous singing of the two halves

STRAW   (0 0)   HAKEA   (0 0)   STERN   (0 0)   WILIWILIA the next one goes further and introduces a completely independent counter-subject, quite separate from any part of the initial melody. This is probably unique in primitive music and of considerable musicological importance. Not only are the two melodies executed separately with perfect harmony (with canonical imitations from time to time), but they are readjusted horizontally so as to give a new vertical alignment that is equally remarkable. Finally the climax is reached by version D: the first and third voices begin together with the countermelody and the second half of the original one, with the second entering a bar later along with the complete original melody. After 12 bars the second melody starts to double the first and third alternately. The conception is of amazing ingenuity, the execution of staggering beauty red perhaps this letter will reach you just before you leave, Marie-Jo darling; I'll risk it. Kisses. I've played some parts of Your Faust; it went off well, with a discussion over a glass of beer, and I'm going back to my room to look at the egg-shaped news on the TV before MS comes for me red backdrop: Easter morning at Hermannsburg showing the old cemetery with the new church and the 90th anniversary cross silhouetted against the dawn. What are you dreaming about Cécile, what are you thinking about? Hymns, motets, canticles, camp fire songs. Far away. Interval: slides of Hermannsburg, Areyonga, Papunya, Alice Springs, the life of choir members red in the dreamtime Nimbawah, accompanied by his two dogs, travelled to a large swamp by the Gudjamandi waterhole and settled down there for the night, what are you dreaming about Agnès, what are you doing, say the people of Oenpelli far, far away, and the next day he walked towards the North as far as Maduluk in the hills where he left his two dogs, then went on alone but got lost in the woods. After much thought, he cut a path through the undergrowth to the Gunjudruk lagoon on whose shore there lived Diundu, his wife Glaramanduik and their many children. Seeing a pigeon-hawk perched on a tree, Nimbawah told him that he was tired of being a man

LYRE-BIRD   (O O)   NGALOIT   (O O)   QUEENSLAND   (O O)   BANDICOOT if only he could become a barramundi in that cool, delicious water, and this occurred. Glaramanduik saw him, threw a stick, and missed. Nimbawah caused the lagoon to swell considerably, and the woman, not knowing what was going on, tried once more to kill him. The barramundi flooded Diundu's camp. She tried again, whereupon Nimbawah created so much water that she was engulfed and tried to swim free. But the barramundi transformed himself into a rainbow-serpent, drowned her, then got out of the water, put her on his shoulders and fled. In a safe place he transformed himself into a great pillar of rock and Glaramanduik became a bulge on his side. The children saw the flood coming and tried to make a barrage of stones. But the water swallowed them up just as their father Diundu returned from the hunt with a lot of dead goannas. He was a powerful magician and he took his stone axe to kill Nimbawah, but it was too late, he had already turned to stone. Then he tried to cut off his head, but the axe shattered; then he decided to change himself into a stone pillar in the middle of all his pebble-children so that he would haunt him for ever red we felt unable to copy the figure of the very large jerboa named kangaroo by the natives of the country, which appears in Captain Cook's first voyage, because it appears to us to be too faulty, but we must relate here what the famous navigator had to say about this strange animal which up to now has never been found except on the continent of New Holland: as I was walking in the morning a short way from the vessel red on the back of the brown, green, orange and yellow $A50 note, next to library shelves, stained-glass windows and bacterial cultures, the portrait of Florey. What are you dreaming about Mathilde? EB: Howard Walter, baron (1898-), Australian pathologist, 1945 Nobel Prize for physiology and medicine with Ernst Chain and Sir Alexander Fleming for the discovery of penicillin

BARK   (0 0)   GREVILLEA   (0 0)   COMPASSES   (0 0)   NALUK and its curative properties for various infectious diseases red how do you translate Australia into French? What are you looking at, Cècile, what are you dreaming about? There are very few books in our language about this country; it's like a blind spot on the other side. I only know of the fine texts by Jules Verne in Captain Grant's Children and Mistress Branican. So I feel like a pioneer. My second journey of discovery, after New Zealand, began in Brisbane, and it was in QLD that I first encountered Australian nature. The first time I was only in planes and capital cities—no kangaroos, koalas, orchids or tree-grass, very few wattles or eucalypts, only a few beautiful Aboriginal artifacts in a museum—but this time I was greeted by rainforests, banksias, crimson rosellas. I had a week's holiday in the Centre. A few years previously, the editor of a French journal had asked me to organize a special issue for him, which I did with a few friends. We were allowed two colour plates: one was used for a Chinese cut-out representing a mask from the former Peking Opera, the other for a photograph of Ayers Rock at Sunset, and I felt morally obliged to go and see with my own eyes this navel of Australian strangeness. So I flew with a friend from Melbourne to Alice Springs, where we hired a car and plunged into the redness. I got to know Australian beer, began to compare the brands in the unique atmosphere of the pubs, sent some books back to France, and a few years went by. I was always thinking of Australia, I was always very excited when I talked about it, but unable to write anything at all about it. That's why I had to come back a third time to become slightly Australian myself, to remain for a few weeks in the same place, explore its surroundings, let them become familiar; I was therefore very happy when the University of QLD gave me the opportunity red landed at 38°S on the eastern part of New Holland, sailed Northward up the coast, anchoring and exploring on several occasions until 10 June, when they hit a rock

KANGAROO   (0 0)   NARAMA   (0 0)   TASMANIA   (0 0)   KOALA in an area where it will be seen that I had considerable difficulties myself; they remained fast for 23 hours and spent two months making repairs in a little port near the rock that had almost caused their deaths BOUGAINVILLE after being in danger on several occasions in these deadly regions they finally found at 10°S a strait between New Holland and the lands of New Guinea through which they entered the Indian Sea red in September at Toowoomba far away, don't miss the flower festival red the people of Canberra go on to tell how when Yarralumla House was sold to the government a letter was found, recounting the whole story and ending with these words: the diamond is with the Aborigine's bones. It is priceless. Far, far away. My hand enfeebled with age prevents me from describing the trials I have undergone. I have lost my life, squandered my money, and I die destitute in sight of my goal. I believe the grave to be under a large deodar tree. As it was dug by the Aborigines from this area, it would be a round hole. I bequeath the fortune which eludes me to the person who will believe me. Unsigned red restless fly-catcher, often found around house windows looking for insects; black-backed magpie, the buzzing is made by flies at the end of the world red now a brief description of the port or river in which we anchored at the other end COOK and which I named after our ship red as discreet as the mimi of Australian myth who at the slightest alert breathe on a crack in the rock until it opens to let them through on the other side of the other changing end of the red world BRETON they play on the ephemeral and work by enchantment red little Francis has been to Papunya and has painted it as a brown hut beneath a brown sun far away, with the landscape reduced to a big black point red the morning star on the back of a bark painting: each evening its guardian lets it out of the bag in which it is imprisoned, and it shows the dead the way to Earth so that at night they can let their relatives know how they are, far, far away, and as he has it on a long string, he brings it back in the morning, when all the dead follow it back to their home in paradise red and there will still be

PAPER (0 0) VERTICORDIA (0 0) NET (0 0) TIMARA

at least a few lines missing on Granny Smith apples, the Matilda Waltzers' Union at the end of the world, the five bars, each corresponding to a social class, at the Stuart Arms in Alice Springs, and the desert nicknames red long green swards stretched out beneath the clumps of trees in Captain Grant's Children; except that a few regular swellings in the ground divided them into divisions that were still quite visible, like a vast chessboard at the other changing end of the red world. Paganel was not deceived by the sight of this wilderness, so poetically arranged for eternal rest VERNE he recognized the funerary plots whose last vestiges the grass is today obliterating, and which the traveller encounters so seldom on Australian soil. "The groves of death," he said red the second supplementary card lists the articles returned to the French department on the other side, with the caption: Coolangatta-Kirra QLD with the Tweed River in the background on the Gold Coast red molten lava pouring from Kilauea Iki, Hawaii, on the wall of my room in college red new arrivals on the goldfields: distance tells, as the jackaroo, as he is called, finds out when he arrives on the diggings. Believing himself to be an experienced miner, but without adapting his dress, he has scorned the idea of going on horseback, and sets out on a long journey on foot. Far away. Many are so disheartened by the difficulties or so yearn for home that they return to Melbourne considering that they know quite enough about goldmines and determined never again to give up the quill for the shovel. As a young man puts it in a colonial ballad: I've got to work with all my might/ and throw up nasty clay/ if my mother could but see me now/ whatever would she say red when one of us dies and the spirits have presented him to the chief of the dead, say the people of Yirrkala far, far away, the chief explains how to make a special wooden canoe, and when it is finished, they both set out for Nalkuma with seeds given by the spirits which will serve as a passport red when in 1861 the convicts began to build the asylum which is today Fremantle Museum at the red end of the changing world, there were already locked up in a warehouse 16 imperial lunatics (convicts), six colonial lunatics

EMU   (0 0)   GURUGADJI   (0 0)   NORTHERN TERRITORY   (0 0)   BARRAMUNDI one convicted colonial lunatic, nine colonial female lunatics red what is the meaning of old age and death for the Aborigines? Old people are looked after by their descendants who respect them for their wisdom and knowledge at the other end. Numerous and varied mourning and funeral rites serve above all to ensure the spirit's safe passage to the land of the dead in the sky, on an island or at a totemic site, and to protect the living from his displeasure, often by avenging him red the people of Yirrkala believe that in the dreamtime two brothers went fishing on a river near Blue Mud Bay and caught a cod near an island, but that on the way back they ran into a terrible storm which smashed their canoe on the other side, and they swam towards land for hours, and that then the arms of the youngest swelled up so much because he had forgotten to take off his armbands that he lost consciousness and drowned; the elder brother managed to reach a rock, but was too exhausted to reach the nearest shore; their bodies were found on a pebbly beach where the ants, who had heard what had happened, came in long lines to bite them in the vain hope of awakening them; meanwhile the river had become the Milky Way where the spirits of all men meet again in eternity red are you looking for romance or friendship? You must feel very lonely, don't be shy, don't stay at home on your own, life is too short, unmarrieds, widows, divorcees, separated women or unmarried mothers with nowhere to go to make new friends, let our very respectable club look after you whatever your age red by dialling a number in Sydney far away, you can get the time red Magnetic Island abounds with bushland settings so superbly untouched that you feel you're the first person there far, far away, on foot or on a hired motorbike, whichever you prefer, the island your compass-needle swings to red political awareness is increasing in the desert, you can read at the Opal Centre at the end of the world, and if the electoral boundaries are not too unfavourable for rural inhabitants

WOOD   (o o)   NUYTSIA   (o o)   SCULPTOR   (o o)   GRADAU it is likely that the Black Australians will soon have not merely the right to participate in the government of this country, but also the means red how far have you got John McNeil at the other end, what has happened to your dream red no two opals are exactly alike at the other end and what an investment red the bunyip according to John Morgan's informants, kisses, laid cunning traps for women red ginnie = Aboriginal woman; girlie = white woman red *vocabulary* (0 0) LETTERS FROM THE ANTIPODES (0 0) *the principality* the inhabitants of a village in WA have set up an independent state named Hutt River Province under the leadership of Leonard Casley, who calls himself Prince Leonard. He has a court, creates knighthoods, has a customs post at the frontier, issues passports and notes whose value is guaranteed by the combined wealth of the principality's inhabitants deposited in a Sydney bank. Tourism flourishes. He has just put into circulation silver dollars bearing his effigy, minted in Canada. The federal government is beginning to tire of the joke, but isn't sure what to do red silvie = silver dollar; kisses; custie = customs officer red lucky or unlucky stone at the end of the world, a whole rush in one opal red the Melbourne Argus of 23 June 1894 explains that the dull roaring heard by marshes at night and which is attributed to the bunyip at the other end, is merely the call of the red Australian bittern red how far have you got, Toby Ginger, other world, what's become of your dream red by dialling a number in Sydney far away, you'd be able to hear the weather red Green Island, you're right on a coral platform where all the living wonders of the Great Barrier Reef invite you for days of exploration in the waters or through the windows of Marineland Melanesia where you can view the beauties and dangers of the deep, seen normally by only the most daring of divers. Dive deep down into the underwater sky of Green Island red the people of Yirrkala believe that the Magellan Clouds are the homes of two sisters and their dogs and that during the dry season the elder one goes away to show her disapproval of the younger who having said one day that she was going to defecate in the bush

OPOSSUM   (0 0)   ANIAUTJUNU   (0 0)   VICTORIA   (0 0)   WOMBAT simply came back with three children to whom she had just given birth, but in the wet season she allows herself to be moved and returns to help her family red come out of your shell at the other changing end of the inverted world, we have a match for you red of course I have been to the asylum, the mayor of Fremantle told us, I used to cross the camel-track on the hill and go and play cricket there. Some years ago I took the director of the new psychiatric hospital up there. He was surprised when I showed him the old hot room, he'd never heard of anything like it, a little stone room for inmates who became violent. They were treated by lighting a big fire underneath, and it seems that they soon calmed down red what is the future of the Aborigines? Other world red the discovery of gold or rewarded at last: after having been reduced far away to the direst straits of poverty red when one of us dies and journeys to Nalkuma, say the people of Yirrkala far, far away, its inhabitants who are expecting him send an expedition to kill a dugong for the feast, while others light a large grass fire whose smoke guides the travellers. When they appear on the horizon, the inhabitants gather on the shore and welcome them. The closest friends of the newcomer embrace him, then he is settled in, with eating, singing and dancing, setting up clouds of dust that rise into the sky and set off storms to let us know that our mourning is over red the last supplementary card is about a borrowed recording of Les Indes galantes which I was unable to listen to down under, with the caption: frangipani red America stopped Columbus on his way to the Orient, completing the journey round the map, 21 years later Vasco Nunez de Balboa impressively broke through that continental barrier when, from the mountains of Panama, he was the first European to see the Eastern Pacific red there will still be at least a few lines missing on racehorses, the gallery for the blind in the Brisbane art museum, the lights called minmin that are supposedly sometimes seen in the desert

BRICK   (0 0)   CALYTHRIX   (0 0)   SHIELD   (0 0)   NALJANIO and also red a native cemetery lay there before his eyes, but so cool, so shady, so enlivened by birds gaily taking wing, so inviting that it awakened no sad thoughts. It could easily have been taken for a Garden of Eden, when death was banished from Earth. Other world. It seemed made for the living VERNE but the tombs, which the savage looked after with pious care, were already disappearing beneath a rising tide of greenery. The conquest had driven the Australian far from the land where his ancestors rested, and colonization would soon be handing these fields of death over to herds for pasture. Thus these groves have become rare, and many which are already trodden by the indifferent traveller, conceal an entire recent generation red little Sandra has been to Alice Springs far away. What a crowd! What a whirl! What blue red panorama on the back of a bark painting: it is what Banumbirr the morning star far away sees on his nightly journey red may man, with the difficulty he has in surviving today, here take measure of his lost powers at the end of the world, and may he who, in the midst of general alienation, resists his own alienation BRETON turn back on himself like the Australian boomerang LAUTREAMONT in the second phase of its flight red back home at The Antipodes at the other end, I'm listening to Les Indes galantes red bittern on the other brown side red and as it was probable that we would land no more on this coast of New Holland on the other side of the other dawning end of the faraway lost world without end, I hoisted English colours COOK and in the name of His Majesty King George III I took possession of the whole eastern coast by the name of New South Wales red when in Toowoomba don't miss the carnival of flowers far away with the help of the camera obscura red the people of Canberra go on to tell how the grounds of Yarralumla House have been dug over many times, and that in spite of all official denials the phantom of the Aborigine, with his diamond shining like the morning star inside his rib cage, nightly disturbs the sleep of the Queen's respresentative red within the spectrum of reality a new colour is appearing right here, at the end of the latent world, distilled by the proximity of the great central exterior, and soon everyone everywhere will need it along with the others to create his palette

ECHIDNA   (0 0)   BIWIT   (0 0)   GOANNA   (0 0)   STONE red and finally landed at the Downs BOUGAINVILLE having enriched the world by a great amount of geographical knowledge at the other end of the rediscovered world, and by interesting discoveries in the three realms of nature red finally my lieutenant, Mr Gore, while out walking in the country with his rifle a few days later, on the other side of the other distant end of the other dawning world COOK was lucky enough to kill one of these quadrupeds which had so often been the subject of our speculation red on the back of the $A50 note next to a mixture of clumps of grass, molecular diagrams, radiotelescope, snow crystals, electrocardiogram, computer dial, bee, microscope, etc., the portrait of Clunies-Ross. The EB has only this: family, since 1886 proprietors of the Cocos Islands in the Indian Ocean, under Australian mandate since 1955, population approximately 600 servants red in the deamtime, say the people of Oenpelli far, far away, Buruk reminded Kurabara as they were sitting round a camp fire on one of their jaunts that he had promised to make a painting of him. "I'll lie on the ground, so that you can study me. Paint what you see." When he had finished, Buruk was so pleased that he offered to paint Kurabara, but Kurabara wanted to see not only his external form, but also the heart, lungs, spine, all the important bits. When the painting was finished, the two friends who until then had believed they were just men, saw that they were a dingo and a kangaroo, which delighted them. They remained for a while in the same place, then set up camp in a cave in the hills where they did such beautiful new paintings that they became identical with them red this morning it's raining heavily, Marie-Jo darling; I put on my boots, light overalls and raincoat to go to the supermarket for bread and jam. I've got to go to the department. Have a good trip, relax in the planes. We'll be waiting for you at Sydney airport on the morning of the fourth

BLACK BOY   (0 0)   ELIXIR   (0 0)   FLYING FISH   (0 0)   OPAL

Afterword

I. Travel and Writing

There are many ways of travelling, just as there are many ways of writing. Some of the former are set out in the essay by Butor whose title is reproduced at the head of this section.[1] One of the most interesting forms of travel is obviously exploration, and to travel as an explorer is to inscribe, writes Butor, since one either leaves physical evidence of where one has been, for instance by planting a flag, or by naming the place concerned on a map (frequently both forms of inscription are used). For Butor the writer-traveller, "to travel . . . in a certain way is to write (and firstly because to travel is to read), and to write is to travel", and the form that writing takes is to reproduce or amend a certain itinerary, to choose or avoid certain cities or sites. Gérard de Nerval's *Voyage en Orient* is radically different from Chateaubriand's *Itinéraire de Paris à Jérusalem*, he continues, since Nerval carefully avoids the latter's key stages: Rome, Athens, Jerusalem, substituting Cairo, Beirut and Constantinople as a means of denouncing the "lie" proposed by the accepted Western cultural and religious tradition represented by these three cities, and confronting it with an occult interpretation based on other centres. But if Nerval's strategy is initially one of avoidance, amendment is equally fruitful: "The terms Rome, Athens, Jerusalem, set out in a certain order by the phase of my journey, can be greatly varied, according to what I have learnt from it, in my account of it, and hence I can discover a multitude of passages and diagonals."

To write (about travel) is thus to set up a dialogue of places, recreating and commenting on the relationship between them or creating new relationships by altering the order and manner of their presentation. A further dimension of complexity is added by Butor's concept of the place or "site": if it is a focal point of diachronic forces (architectural, cultural, religious, etc.), it also has a strong synchronic element, since it is "the focal point of a horizon of other places, the point of origin of a series of possible routes passing through other more or less determined regions. In my town many other towns are present through a variety of intermediaries: direction signs, geography books, things coming from them, newspapers talking about them, pictures and films which show them to me, my memories of them, novels which make me pass through them".[2] If Butor is here emphasising what might be called the "receptive" nature of the focal point, it is obvious that all places also possess a "radiating" power which is more or less strong according to the individual's cultural or affective makeup. For example, the "radiating" power of Paris is presumably strong for a francophile (unless he dislikes large cities), while that of Sydney is non-existent in this respect. To somebody born in Sydney and living in Paris, the converse is probably true.

Boomerang and, within it, "Letters from the Antipodes", is the latest of a series of texts juxtaposing historical sites, cities, or countries in an attempt better to understand "the spirit of the place" (le génie du lieu). The first in the series, simply named *Le Génie du lieu* (Paris: Grasset, 1958), treats a variety of Mediterranean cities and sites: Cordoba, Istanbul, Salonika, Delphi, Mallia, Mantua, Ferrara; and a Mediterranean country: Egypt (mainly the small town of El Minya, where the young Butor spent some time attempting to teach French). The historico-cultural dimension, what Butor calls the "depth of a city" (p.51), is given great importance, and the radiating power of cities such as Rome (p.97, section on Mantua) is occasionally stressed. But as far as their presentation within the space of the book is concerned, the cities and sites remain essentially isolated from each other.

With *Où, le génie du lieu, 2*, Butor both widens his geographical horizons (Paris, various places in the United States, Seoul, Angkor-Wat) and begins to utilize the physical resources of the book-as-object,[3] with one of the sections—a series of attempts to describe a range of mountains seen through a window—continuously invaded by material from others. In other words, both thematic and visual "contamination" occur, since the surface of the page provides a background for the juxtaposition of material differentiated by the use of various kinds and sizes of type, indentation, and so on. Within the successive framework of the book (one can still follow the text straight through from beginning to end, although other reading journeys are possible) a certain simultaneity of presentation has been achieved. Numerous other texts written in the sixties and seventies (*Mobile*: the United States; *6 810 000 Litres d'eau par seconde*: the Niagara Falls; *Description de San Marco*: St Mark's, Venice) also weave together disparate textual strands on the same page to form a series of *collages* proposing a series of itineraries for the reader-explorer. When we read we (re)write;[4] when we write we travel; when we travel we write: so that our own exploration/rewriting does not become "errance" (wandering), we must now take careful note of the textual landmarks within *Boomerang*.

148

In a famous essay entitled "Le Livre, instrument spirituel" (The Book as Spiritual Instrument),[5] the poet Stéphane Mallarmé contrasts the raw immediacy of the newspaper with the ideal book, "total expansion of the letter . . . mobility", a kind of musical score, with a core phrase in large characters surrounded by subsidiary groups in smaller type, "a scattering of fioritura". Some seventy years later, Butor's concept of the book-as-object develops Mallarmé's reflections:

> The book, as we understand it today, is . . . the arrangement of the thread of the discourse within a three-dimensional space, according to a double measure: length of line, depth of page, an arrangement which has the advantage of allowing the reader great freedom of movement in relation to the "unfolding" of the text, great mobility, an arrangement which is as close as possible to a simultaneous presentation of all parts of a work.[6]

The book, Butor writes elsewhere, has a great advantage over printed material such as the microfilm in that its pages can be turned forwards and backwards with ease, allowing "browsing".[7] *Boomerang* is the latest major work by Butor to treat the page and the typographic character not as constraints but as aids in the simultaneous presentation of material, which in turn engenders what might provisionally be called thematic encounters. But the major structuring force, working with typographic and visual elements, is the use of a rigid serial framework which governs the order in which the various sections appear (see graph 1). In turn, within each section, further patterns of arrangement and thus of contiguity are created. Butor's aesthetic of juxtaposition, which has strong affinities with the poetic procedures of the Surrealists, sets up an equilibrium between hetero- and homogeneity, fluidity and rigidity characteristic of the more successful "open" or "serial" text, to use a terminology to which I shall return later.[8]

Boomerang comprises seven interwoven sections as follows (in the order in which they first appear): "Jungle"; "The Ceremony I Missed"; "Letters from the Antipodes"; "Nouvelles [New] Indes Galantes"; "Bicentenary Kit"; "Transatlantic Carnival"; "Archipelago Shopping". The total length of the sections varies considerably: "Letters from the Antipodes" is formed of twenty-four blocks of text of between four and seven pages (144 pages total: the original pagination has been kept in the translation as a reminder of how it is divided); next comes "Archipelago Shopping" (fourteen blocks, ninety-six pages), then "Bicentenary Kit" twelve, eighty) followed by "The Ceremony I Missed" (nine, forty-eight) and "Transatlantic Carnival" (ten, forty-eight), "Nouvelles Indes Galantes" (twelve, twenty-four) and finally "Jungle" (eight, sixteen). The eighty-

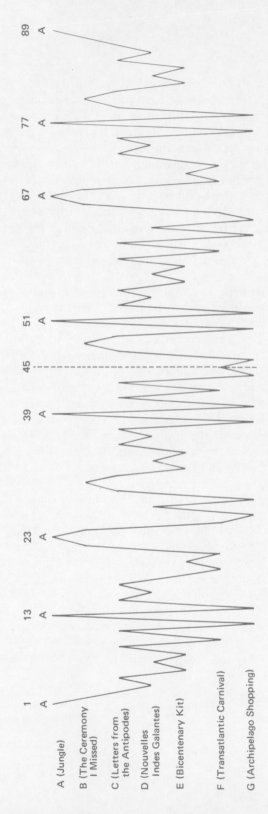

A (Jungle)

B (The Ceremony
I Missed)

C (Letters from
the Antipodes)

D (Nouvelles
Indes Galantes)

E (Bicentenary Kit)

F (Transatlantic Carnival)

G (Archipelago Shopping)

Graph 1. Order of the seven sections and eighty-nine textual blocks of *Boomerang*. The distribution is almost regular.

nine sections, forming a total of 456 pages (pagination starts at page five), are ordered almost symmetrically, with for instance the end of the book reversing the order of the beginning: ABCDCEDEC/CEDECDCBA (see graph 1). The pattern of contiguities thus created engenders a series of geographic and textual echoes and encounters: for example, "Archipelago Shopping" (G) is most frequently juxtaposed with "Letters from the Antipodes" (twelve times) and "Jungle" (eight), but does not come into immediate contact with "Bicentenary Kit".

A second pattern which partly overlaps with the first is provided by the use of three colours of type: red, black and blue; again, these are not distributed at random, since two basic rules are observed. The first, imposed by the printer for reasons of cost, is simply that each colour block (there are twenty-nine in all) forms sixteen consecutive pages. The second, Butor's, is that no one colour shall be used in two consecutive sixteen page blocks. A third "rule", which engenders encounters rather different from those obtained by the overall ordering of the eighty-nine sections, is the ordering of sections within each colour block. The overall order is of course not changed, but in the case of "Archipelago Shopping", for example, within the coloured blocks it becomes a "framing" section, along with "Bicentenary Kit" and "Letters from the Antipodes". Conversely, other sections are framed (see graph 2). Colour is also one means whereby a section is characterized. Red is predominant (twelve colour blocks out of twenty-nine), followed by black (nine) and blue (eight). "Letters from the Antipodes" is always red, "Jungle" is always black, and "Bicentenary Kit" blue, whereas the four other sections change colour according to how they are distributed within the overall pattern.

Each section is further characterized visually in three basic ways. First, all pages of the section are composed typographically in the same manner. To give three examples: "Jungle" (black) forms a textual block in the centre of the page; "The Ceremony I Missed" comprises two ten-line textual blocks, one at the top of the page and one at the bottom, separated by a large blank space in the middle of which is a running title in capitals; "Letters from the Antipodes" has its textual block situated towards the top of the page, with a substantial blank space below and the running title beneath it. The number of lines per block can vary within certain limits—between twenty-two and thirty-five lines in the case of "Letters from the Antipodes"—thus giving sufficient "margin" for the series of thematic elements to form a coherent and self-motivated whole having the same kind of relation with the rest of the book as an individual poem has with a *structured* compilation of poems (for example *Les Fleurs du Mal* by Baudelaire). Within each visual block the type is normally in roman,

151

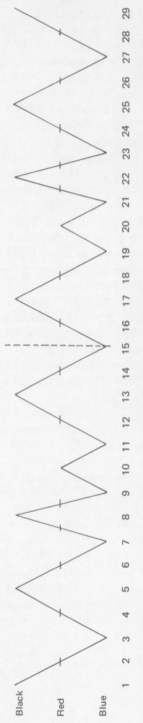

Graph 2. Distribution of colour blocks of sixteen pages. Numbers indicate the twenty-nine colour blocks, each of sixteen pages, making up the 464 pages of *Boomerang*. The distribution is perfectly regular.

but some use is made of italic, while capitalization indicates sources. The running titles characterizing each section are formed of various elements. To take what is probably the most complex example, "Transatlantic Carnival" (text in middle of page, running titles top and bottom), they bring together five lists: the twenty states of Brazil, twenty parts of the body, twenty-four "carnival words" ("cries", "laughter", "crackers", "garlands", and so on), twelve Old Testament prophets and fourteen "carnival accessories". Constellations are also frequently used ("The Ceremony I Missed", "Letters from the Antipodes"). Finally, each series of lists is punctuated by a special sign, for example ($) for "Bicentenary Kit", and (0 0) for "Letters from the Antipodes" (see translation p.371 for explanation).

Like "Letters from the Antipodes", all the other sections are composed of a series of "thematic" or "source" strands, frequently taking the form of lists, the most notable example being "Archipelago Shopping" (currencies, foods, sightseeing curiosities), and the manner of their juxtaposition within the visual, geographic and mathematical framework of the whole book—and, within the book, each section and block—is at first difficult to follow. For example, early on in "The Ceremony I Missed", the upper section of the page brings together various elements associated with the state of Washington and British Columbia: a series of Northwest Coast Indian legends as transcribed by Claude Lévi-Strauss, and what are basically travel anecdotes. These are juxtaposed with other elements in the lower section of the page associated with the United States and in particular the Shalako Indian ceremonies. After a time, however, certain upper and lower elements change place and for a period the Canadian pieces take over the whole text, before equality is restored in the final section.

It should already be clear that the combination of three colours, seven sections, and pages containing two blocks of text is an invitation to abandon the beaten track of page-after-page sequential reading for byways of textual exploration which may entail jumping many pages, only reading part of them, and so on. "Archipelago Shopping" virtually imposes the byways, since the two blocks of text per page allow four different versions of the section as a whole to unfold, and if any sequentiality at all is desired, then the reader must follow each version on *alternate* pages—except at certain points in the book where they cross over (pp. 140,326).

3. Boomerang: The Sections

Among the seven sections of *Boomerang*, two—"Jungle" and "Nouvelles Indes Galantes"—form a kind of contrasting accompaniment to the rest.[9] The first—

based on Buffon's *Natural History*—frames the whole book (pp. 5–6 and 459–60), providing a note of refined savagery which cannot be subsumed in any simple manner under the nature/culture opposition, since *Boomerang's* darkest Africa is doubly literary, Buffon's descriptions of its fauna being heavily rewritten by Butor. The contrast with "Nouvelles Indes Galantes" is nonetheless considerable, since to the doubly-literary treatment of the pieces on animals, the first-named piece opposes the excessively cultural text formed by Butor's recasting of Fuzelier's words to Rameau's heroic ballet (hence the "*New* Indes Galantes") in four scenes (Turkey, Peru, Persia, North America). To the obvious geographical contrast is allied the differing protocols of language: Buffon/Butor's description of the hunting, eating and copulatory habits of various animals and the bittern provides a foil for the hyper-refined language of courtship in the imaginary world of eighteenth-century art (Buffon and Rameau were contemporaries).

The remaining five pieces have in common the utilization of material drawn from various geographical regions and cultures—as opposed to the imaginary world of Rameau and the world without man of Buffon. "The Ceremony I Missed" has already been briefly described; like the four other "real" geographical sections it is characterized by an art-form (in this case the totem-pole) and, like "Letters from the Antipodes", it is much concerned with native legend and custom: here, the Potlatch ceremony. The rôle of money and exchange in *Boomerang* would repay careful study, with the economy of the Potlatch (described in a text by Georges Bataille)[10] very different in its implications from the use and presentation of money in "Bicentenary Kit" (the $ sign, references to the Wall Street Crash, etc.), in "Archipelago Shopping" (the currencies) or in "Letters from the Antipodes" ("bibliography of banknotes").

"Bicentenary Kit" is formed of fifty texts of Butor, including eighteen referring to a series of silk-screen paintings by Jacques Monory and thirty-two commenting on various other texts and objects which, together with the Monory paintings and Butor's texts, make up the contents of a homage to Marcel Duchamp in the form of a transparent box produced to mark the bicentenary of the United States.[11] The pieces undergo various transformations, the most radical of which consists of the addition of extracts from Butor's *Mobile*, which dialogue with the *Bicentenary Kit* extracts to form a series of prose-poems on the various American states (real and projected). Like the rest of the book, "Bicentenary Kit" is doubly-removed from any "reality", since it re-uses other texts which are in some sense or other related to that reality—except that elsewhere they are by other writers, whereas in this section they are by Butor. The implications of this will be considered in part 6.

"Archipelago Shopping", ostensibly set in Singapore, uses the city's position as a crossroads of the Pacific—and arguably the whole Eastern world—to introduce various other places in the Pacific region (Tahiti, Japan, Los Angeles, Australia, New Caledonia) seen through the eyes of explorers or literary personalities (Bougainville, Diderot, Melville, Segalen, the Marquis de Sade of *Sainville et Léonore*), and an earlier Butor, in the form of reworked parts of a "radiophonic text" entitled *Réseau aérien*. A powerful dimension of sexuality is imparted by the use of various pieces on Tahiti, Bougainville's "New Cythera" where Cook observed the transit of Venus. The code of conduct which the English missionary David Oire made King Pomaré II and thirty-one chiefs sign in 1820 excluded all forms of "illicit" sexual activity; in Butor's text it is interwoven with extracts from Bougainville and others describing the unabashed, rampant sexuality of the natives before what Alan Moorehead has named "the fatal impact"[13] of white civilization began to take effect (*Boomerang*, pp. 75 *passim*).

"Transatlantic Carnival" is made up of twenty pieces ("floats") relating to certain European cities—Nice, Mallia, Geneva, Rome—and a variety of locations in South America. Nearly all are reworked texts by a variety of authors including Butor himself (for example "Mallia" from *Le Génie du lieu*, and a poem full of humour and malice entitled "Salade niçoise"). Not surprisingly, all three colours are used for this section, and the work of art characterizing it is the carnival float itself. Like "Archipelago Shopping", it proposes a plurality of itineraries set out on alternate pages, with cross-over points. Finally, more than any other section perhaps it exemplifies the dialogue and co-presence of places, with constant contrasts with, and echoes and reminders of "elsewhere".[14]

4. *"Letters from the Antipodes": Structure*

"Letters from the Antipodes" is by far the most important part of this geographical, literary and onomastic mosaic, not only by virtue of its length but because it is arguable that the contaminatory effect works outward more than inward as far as it is concerned. In other words, it is more "radiating" than "receptive", with its presence—or absence—felt particularly in "Archipelago Shopping". Its colour—red—and typographical disposition have already been described; the running title is placed at the bottom of the page, largely because of one of its elements, the Southern Hemisphere Constellations. Four other elements are used: Australian flora; Australian fauna; the names—real and invented—of wedding anniversaries (see translation, p.307); and, towards the end, names of vari-

155

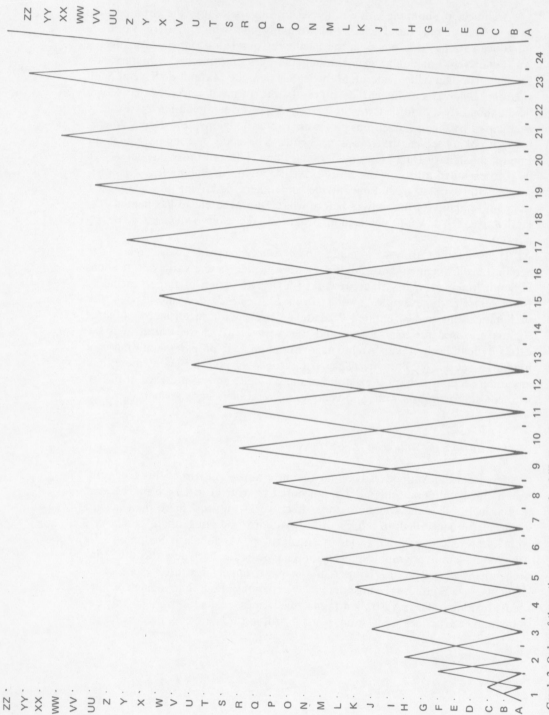

Graph 3. Order of thematic or source strands of "Letters from the Antipodes". Numbers refer to the twenty-four textual blocks of "Letters from the Antipodes". For alphabetical key, see pp. 157-58. For commentary on distribution, see pp. 158-60.

ous protagonists of Aboriginal legends. The twenty-four blocks of text are made up of thirty-two or thirty-five different "source strands", depending on how they are counted. Each strand is introduced by its title in italic, with capitals (for example COOK) indicating its provenance. The text also frequently comments on itself, indicating how it may be read, a kind of equivalent to the "directions for use" found on manufactured articles, and one of many ways in which the notion of creative art is demystified.[15] Just as there is an overall structure to *Boomerang*, similarly, within it, "Letters from the Antipodes" is ordered in a complex but regular manner. The general organizing principle is best described in terms of two coexistent numerical or mathematical series, one increasing (1–32 or A–ZZ) and the other decreasing (32–1 or ZZ–A), and is best illustrated in simplified graph form (see graph 3), where each "source strand" has been separately coded alphabetically. Various other principles are immediately apparent. After the first two blocks, which introduce, respectively, six and three strands, only one strand per block is subsequently introduced, with the exception of block five (L + M); in very general terms, the section as a whole is therefore of increasing complexity, since an ever-increasing number of strands is available for permutation. In specific terms, the actual complexity varies, with a change occurring from block thirteen on. Until then, strands are added only; from block thirteen they can be left out (the one exception is D (dreams) of which there are only six). This phenomenon is most marked in the last few sections: block twenty-four is a kind of recapitulation or coda, using all strands except D, giving a total of fifty-five segments (a strand may appear several times in any given block); this is however preceded by three blocks (twenty-one to twenty-three) each characterized by the absence of a large number of strands: D and I–U in twenty-one; A,C,E,G,H,O,V–XX and Y–WW in twenty-two; and D, K–U and W–X in twenty-three.

In general terms, what might be called the "middle strands" are omitted more frequently than the others, except that it must also be remembered that, because of the principle of adding only one strand per block, the overall tendency within the basic series A–ZZ is for each additional strand to be less important, in terms of the number of times it appears, than preceding ones. The decrease is almost constant from N–ZZ, while the first half dozen strands (with the exception of D again) all recur thirty times or more.[16] In terms of the page, the overall serial or counter-serial organization produces two basic patterns. For pages that are central to each block, for example the middle three pages of a seven-page group, early and late strands tend to be juxtaposed (e.g. section fifteen), or middle ones (section sixteen). For the first and last page of each block, the same kind of phenomenon occurs: pages 149 and 156, which are respectively the last page

of block seven and the first of block eight, are characterized by a grouping
of middle strands, whereas on pages 160 (block eight) and 179 (block nine)
the opposite is the case, with early and late strands occurring. One micro-
grouping is also found, with "the national stone" (Q) and the "red and black
day" (R) invariably appearing close together, whereas in theory either one could
be omitted without seriously disrupting the general pattern.

Within the macro-structure of *Boomerang*, the micro-structure of "Letters
from the Antipodes" thus sets up in turn a whole series of possibilities for thematic encounters of a general and a more specific nature: general, in the sense
that each separate source can be reduced to one or a very limited number of
themes (the first (A) concerns a narrator invited to the University of Queensland
as writer-in-residence, his various explorations, and his preliminary work towards
writing a book about his stay); specific, in that various strands may contain
common elements (for example, the theme of exploration occurs in many).
Further than this, a whole network of motivated phonic, syntactic and metaphorical correspondences and contrasts can be uncovered: "Letters from the Antipodes" is of extraordinary density, richness and coherence, whether treated
as a largely autonomous text or seen in the light of its relationship with other
parts of *Boomerang* (see sections 7.1 and 7.2).

5. *"Letters from the Antipodes": Sources*

The source strands and their provenance are as follows (in the order in which
they appear):

A   *Marie-Jo darling*. Source: a narrator.

B   *Murmurs from Arnhem Land*. Source: Charles Mountford, *Arnhem
     Land Art, Myth and Symbolism*, Melbourne: Melbourne University
     Press, 1956.

C   *bibliography of banknotes*. Sources: *Encyclopedia Britannica*, 1968
     edition; *Dictionary of Australian Biography*, 1949 edition, ed. R. Serle;
     Author and Title Catalogue, University of Queensland Main Library;
     Subject Catalogue, University of Queensland Main Library.

D   *red bicentenary dream* etc. Source: a narrator.

E   *prelude to Cook*. Source: Bougainville, *Voyage autour du monde, par
     la frégate du roi La Boudeuse, discours préliminaire*, Paris, 1772.

F   *ghosts*. Source: W. Fearn-Wannan, *Australian Folklore, A Dictionary
     of Lore, Legends and Popular Allusions*, Melbourne: Lansdowne Press,
     1970.

G   *reconnaissance*. Source: Douglas Baglin and Barbara Mullins, *Captain Cook's Australia*, Sydney: Horowitz Publications, 1969.
H   *documents*. Source: a narrator.
I   *labels*. Source: Department of Aboriginal and Islanders' Advancement, Queensland.
J   *the equivocal racism of Uncle Jules*. Sources: Jules Verne, *Les Enfants du capitaine Grant*; *Mistress Branican*.
K   *Australia Unlimited*. Source: Supplement to the *Sydney Morning Herald*, 19 July 1976.
B[1] *the groves of death*. Source: see B.
L   *Unesco exhibition*. Source: *Australian Aboriginal Culture, An Exhibition arranged by the Australian National Committee for UNESCO*, 1953. Sydney: Government Printer, 1965.
M   *small ads*. Sources: *Adelaide Advertiser*, 19 July 1976; *Brisbane Courier-Mail*, 10 July 1976.
N   *islands in the Sun*. Sources: *TAA Holidays: Islands in the Sun and the Great Barrier Reef*, effective 24 January 1976.
O   *health problems*. Source: Melbourne *Age*, 21–24 September 1971.
F[1] *the bunyip*. Source: see F.
P   *vocabulary*. Source: a narrator.
Q   *the national stone*. Sources: various brochures from opal traders.
R   *the red and black day*. Source: pamphlet issued by The National Aborigines' Day Observance Committee, 1972 (text by J. Newfong).
S   *telephone*. Source: the Sydney telephone directory, 1976.
B[2] *Aboriginal astronomy*. Source: see B.
T   *the asylum*. Source: *Fremantle Museum*, published by the Western Australian Museum, n.d.
U   *lithographs*. Source: *Sketches of Australian Life and Scenery, complete in 12 plates*. Produced for Associated Pulp and Paper Mills Ltd. by N. J. Field and Co. Pty Ltd with kind permission of The National Library of Australia, Canberra, 1970.
V   *showbag*. Source: "Brisbane Kit or Writer's in Residence Showbag" (paper bag with handles containing modified postcards ["ready-mades aidés"?] owned by the translator).
W   *gaps*. Source: a narrator.
X   *children's drawings*. Source: paintings by children at Hermannsburg Mission School, N.T., given to Michel Butor at the school in 1971.
Y   *free hand*. Source: "Main première", by André Breton, preface to *Un Art à l'état brut* by Karel Kupka, Lausanne: Eds, Clairefontaine, 1962.

Z   *bird calls*. Source: "Bird Calls from Australia", recorded by Newton Hobbs, RCA records, RCA UPL 1-0096-G.

UU   *memorial to Raymond Roussel*. Sources: a narrator, and *Toowoomba and Darling Downs Tourist Guide*, 1976.

VV   *talk*. Source: ABC "Guest of Honour" talk, given by Michel Butor in 1976.

WW   *appearance of the word kangaroo in French literature*. Source: Buffon, *OEuvres complètes*, 1817–18.

XX   *concert programme*. Source: *Souvenir Brochure. 1967 Tour of Bethlehem Lutheran Church Choir, Hermannsburg Mission, N.T. Commemorating the 90th Anniversary of the Mission's Founding by the Finke River on June 8th, 1877.*

YY   *counterpoint*. Source: "Arnhem Land Music Part II. A Musical Survey", by Trevor A Jones, *Oceania* 26 (1955–56), p.285.

ZZ   *the principality* (Hutt River Province). Source: a narrator.

The author's sources have all been traced and the relevant parts read, for three reasons. First, for the sake of accuracy and authenticity: unless he has changed them on purpose,[17] there seems no reason why titles of books or names of organizations and places should not be faithfully restored. Second, in the case of translated material, to compare the original and the author's version with a view to understanding better the processes of *his* translation and thus to facilitating our retranslation. Third, with a view to classifying them—various classifications are possible and fruitful—and thus understanding better their interplay in the text.

It is clear from the list above that, with the exception of Mountford and one or two creative texts (Verne and Breton), the remaining sources are either works of vulgarization (Fearn-Wannan, Baglin and Mullins, UNESCO Exhibition) or of the nature of pamphlets, brochures, labels and the like. Many virtually impose serial or catalogue presentation: the bark-painting labels and lithographs, for instance, and of these several, as well as the Mountford text, are also descriptions of art-forms. The author's translation of the last-cited is thus four times removed from any "reality", since the original source is not Mountford at all, but the bark paintings which illustrate the legends recounted in his text. To take another example of the same kind of phenomenon, the voyages recounted by Bougainville are not his own, but those of predecessors and contemporaries.

The Australia of "Letters from the Antipodes" can be characterized in two main ways. It is very largely an Australia as seen and presented by the Australian popular imagination, a largely mythical Australia in both its historical and contemporary dimensions, similar in this respect to the America presented in Butor's *Mobile, étude pour une représentation des Etats-Unis*. As such, it is—again like *Mobile*—a "study for a *re*-presentation" of Australia, an assemblage or reassemblage of texts about or produced in Australia, a *rewriting* of *written* Australia. The second-, third- or fourth-hand dimension of Butor's text is not an elaborate literary game, but a consequence of the notion, which is commonsense enough, that a most important dimension of the real world is the way in which it is (re)presented to us by written, visual and oral media. Butor is concerned with all three, although in "Letters from the Antipodes" it is the first two that exercise him. As he puts it in *Répertoire II* (p.88): "The world, in very large part, only appears to us through what we are told about it: conversations, lessons, newspapers, books, etc." However, he continues, we quickly realize that a large part of what we are told is in certain respects "inaccurate" (p.89); a vital role of the literary text is therefore to restructure information (p.90) in such a way as to reveal hitherto unsuspected relationships, thereby enriching us with new perspectives and transforming our submission to the media into positive use of them. The perspectives on Australia revealed by "Letters from the Antipodes" might therefore be seen as windows in the wall of information surrounding us. But they are in no sense definitive perspectives. To regard them as such would be to cloud the windows' precarious transparency, for "reality" and language are continually changing, and the most any work can do is challenge our preconceptions before it is—inevitably—supplanted: like its author, it is unique only in a very restricted sense. A study of quotation may help us more fully to understand why.

6. *Quotation*

The process of quotation is an interesting one. Basically, it involves a series of contrasting operations: disjunction/conjunction, mutilation/grafting,[18] whereby an element is removed from one text and inserted in a new (con)text, which inevitably modifies its sense, just as its presence as a foreign body in the receiving or "host" text will exercise a modifying influence on that text. One of its traditional roles is that of providing authority, a kind of guarantee of seriousness and authenticity, in its turn guaranteed by the curious device known as footnoting.[19] Whether or not a quotation is an invitation to read the text from which it comes depends partly on whether it is supported by footnotes, partly on the kind of footnote involved (an extended footnote may render referral to the text a luxury). Defended by inverted commas, it also denotes an abdication of responsibility on the part of the receiving text ("I didn't write this, somebody more authoritative than me did"): poor undergraduate assignments frequently use any old quotation in a desperate attempt at achieving respectability, and naive or unscrupulous ones may try to achieve it by dropping the inverted commas altogether. Luckily the kind of stylistic tension mentioned in the introduction makes this very easy to spot.

One desirable effect of quotations is that they should reinforce the semantic coherence of the receiving text, which becomes what is known as an "intertext", a coherent assemblage of several texts.[20] Properly chosen, quotations exhibit their foreignness while becoming partially subsumed or assimilated, semantically speaking. They also emphasize the proprietorial nature of the host text, being as it were hired to work for it, with their sole wages the acknowledgment that they really belong to a text owned by someone else: "The discourse is the last refuge of property, doubtless because it is its origin, and it would take more than a cultural revolution to disturb its economy, such is its stability . . ."[21] Or, putting it slightly differently, quotations are a kind of foil to the host text, emphasizing its uniqueness, the fact that it is a coherent body belonging to an author-proprietor. A whole ideology of ownership and transmission is implied by the commercial promotion of books and a certain kind of discourse in newspapers, schools and universities, with its emphasis on greatness, uniqueness, and influence—often via quotation—as a one-way process.

This ideology has received a battering for many years now at the hands of authors such as James Joyce, Ezra Pound, Jorge Luis Borges (*Pierre Ménard, Author of Don Quixote*), and Butor himself. In Borges's short story, Pierre Ménard is attempting to remain himself, and yet, *without copying it*, to write—not rewrite—Cervantes's *Don Quixote*: the same text written by two distinct authors separated by three centuries, and the whole notion of priority at stake. For if the two novels are verbally identical, the second is "almost infinitely richer" than the first because of the historical gap between them: placed in the context of contemporary ideas, those expressed by Ménard are strange and remarkable.[22] In *Boomerang* the inverted commas disappear and there are no notes; the host text (which host text?) is overwhelmed by quoted material, which must form between eighty and ninety per cent of "Letters from the Antipodes". The hierarchy of host and assimilated material is thus reversed (assuming for the moment only that certain strands such as *Marie-Jo darling*, *gaps*, etc. constitute the host text). The work becomes a construct—the more so as it constantly refers to its own mode of fabrication—and any pretence that a text is a transparent means of letting "reality" appear (thereby denying its own existence) is firmly denied.

If the receiving text is devalued, even dissolved, there is therefore a sense in which the "exterior text" (Fr.: "hors-texte") does not exist either, since there is really no longer any frontier between the two;[23] this is particularly true of the special form of quotation constituted by the reworking of one's own material, or "autoquotation". The immediate referral is to Butor's other works, and the procedure might appear to be at once lazy and solipsistic. But Butor's autoquotations are frequently so substantially reworked as to constitute virtually new texts, so that little if any economy of effort is involved: indeed, it is very hard to rewrite oneself, since the existence of apparently finished material can have a paralyzing effect (the ideology of uniqueness is complemented by the equally pervasive notion of completeness). They also frequently form part of texts that are largely composed of *other* texts, and Butor quoting himself may well turn out to be Butor requoting somebody else. The inward or backward movement is therefore at least balanced by an outward one, insofar as inward or outward have any means left in this play of intertextuality.

This raises again the question of the receiving text and with it that of the author. Given the thirty-two or thirty-five textual strata of "Letters from the Antipodes", there is no particular linguistic reason why, for instance, the first one (*Marie-Jo darling*) should be accorded any special status. It is in the first person and provides some kind of narrative thread, but then so do others, for example *reconnaissance*. Only a computer could tell us if it occupies more actual space than any other strand, not that this would be a compelling factor in any case. It disappears and reappears, being entirely absent from blocks fourteen, sixteen, eighteen, twenty and twenty-two and from many pages in other blocks. If it frames the section on Australia, it should be remembered that the whole book is framed, not by any first person narrator, but by a third-person description of the habits of various animals. What is related at the very beginning of "Letters from the Antipodes" as an event in real life: the narrator's problems with his ticket at Nice airport (p.17), is presented as a dream twenty pages later (p.37: "Bicentenary Kit"), as is another "real" scene at Sydney airport, except that on this occasion the "real" event is recounted in "Archipelago Shopping" (p.65), and the dream in "Letters from the Antipodes" (p.87). And if the narrator here *is* in some sense "real", he appears elsewhere in quite different guises and at very different times: "back home at The Antipodes", giving an ABC broadcast, or lamenting the fact that he will not be able to talk about some things, in textual stands designated as separate. It might be objected that there is one essential difference between the *avatars* of a narrator and the rest of "Letters from the Antipodes": the rest is *designated* as quoted material. This is by no means true, since several strata—*bibliography of banknotes, the national stone, the asylum, lithographs, small ads*—are presented in exactly the same way as *Marie-Jo darling*, that is, without capitals indicating their source.

At the very least, then, we should be wary of privileging any particular stratum and a first-person narrator. Michel Butor speaks of a strong autobiographical element in his recent works, including *Boomerang*. This is true, but an over-rapid assimilation of author to text, or vice versa,[24] may cloud the whole issue of what kind of relationship is involved, with the anecdotal displacing the textual, just as the most common error committed by the average reader is to assume that characters in a novel, film or play are real people. This error is of course the lifeblood of traditional novels, films and plays, which foster it by the development of "reality effects" and calculated verisimilitude. But the only possible status of *Marie-Jo darling* vis à vis the other strands of "Letters from the Antipodes" is *textual*; blandly to assimilate a narrator to an author is simply another means of perpetuating the ideology of uniqueness and proprietorship: not only does an author *own* his text, he is *in* it as well, and the separation of the one from the other becomes impossible.[25]

The preceding paragraphs should suggest that this error is difficult to sustain in the case of *Boomerang*. With the dissemination of the narratorial voice, the precariousness of the host text (assuming that *Marie-Jo darling* is the only serious candidate), and the abolition of the frontier between one text and another in the creation of the intertext, the unique—text and author—is displaced by the *collective*. This has long been one of the principal aims of Butor the writer. "A work is always collective", he once wrote,[26] and there is an obvious sense in which this is true, since all works are a cross-roads of other works, whether quoted or consciously or unconsciously subsumed, and also, as Sartre put it in a famous essay, a meeting point of two free consciousnesses, the author's and the reader's.[27] But the practice of quotation and autoquotation in Butor's more recent works, which contributes to the development of the book as a kind of repertory of textual and intertextual journeys, extends the notion of collectivity both in terms of the work itself, which becomes (part of) a plurality of works, and of the reader, whose freedom may exercise itself in ways not thought of by Sartre.[28] Butor's aesthetic of juxtaposition of quoted material organizes certain possibilities for encounters, which it is up to the reader to realize by the itinerary he chooses.

7.1 Encounters and Echoes: Boomerang and "Letters from the Antipodes"

Because of the ease with which it can be excised from *Boomerang* (it would be impossible to amputate *Mobile* or *Où* in the same way, since each page tends to bring together different "sites"), it is all too easy to treat "Letters from the Antipodes" in isolation, especially as it does appear to function more as a radiating than a receiving site in respect of the other parts of the book. Its relationship with them is however assured partly by the carefully structured overall framework, partly by certain "transitions", to use Butor's own term. What follows is an indication of just a few of the ways in which it relates to the parent text.

In terms of general contiguity, it is a "framing" section within its colour block, coming into contact with three other sections: "Nouvelles Indes Galantes" (six times), and "Transatlantic Carnival" and "The Ceremony I Missed" on three occasions each. In general terms, the juxtaposition with the first is contrastive. The contrast is partly of register, partly geographic: the hyper-gallant language and imaginary exoticism of the sites in Rameau as opposed to the more varied but generally far more prosaic style and the real exoticism of "Letters from the Antipodes". The very special register of massage parlour advertisements (pp. 87 and 90) is set against the equally special register of the language of eighteenth century love (pp. 88–89), and the narrator's journey to the hub of Australian exoticism, Ayers Rock (p.439) is juxtaposed with a discussion of the most appropriately exotic place for a particular imaginary scene (p.440). The three framed parts of "Transatlantic Carnival" are in large part concerned with the impact of European civilization on Paraguay, thus setting up echoes with strands in the Australian section such as the extracts from Jules Verne (compare "Transatlantic Carnival" pp. 310–15 with "Letters from the Antipodes" p.316 and elsewhere). In "The Ceremony I Missed", the framed parts are predominantly concerned with Northwest Coast Indian legends, inviting the reader to constrast them with Aboriginal myths. What is striking about the former is that they invariably end with the enrichment in perpetuity of the locality where they occur; whereas the notion of abundance is unknown to the Aborigine, and the most common word in his vocabulary, according to Verne, is "hunger" (pp. 188–89).

In terms of the book as a whole, without reference to colour, "Letters from the Antipodes" is juxtaposed most frequently with "Archipelago Shopping" (twelve times) and "Bicentenary Kit" (ten), but not at all with "Jungle". Relative geographical proximity and commercial contact are partially responsible in the first case, plus the curious semi-contrast between a basically European civilization settled in the East (Australia) and an Eastern people adopting European customs and commercial practices so successfully that "for years, the European who wanted to see the future had to go to the United States. Today, it would be rather Singapore" ("Archipelago Shopping", p.400). The contaminatory effect of "Letters from the Antipodes" is so strong that certain incidents occurring in Australia are related within "Archipelago Shopping". In "Archipelago Shopping 3" (p.143) the narrator tells his wife that they will do their duty-free shopping at Singapore, but "Archipelago Shopping 1" (p.195) relates how this intention is thwarted at Brisbane airport, half the money that had been put aside for this purpose being used to pay for excess baggage.

A similar kind of semi-contrast with the United States may also be discerned: two "New Worlds", with a widespread mythology of presidents in the one (the series entitled *presidential napkins, even*) and the even more widespread non-mythology of the largely unknown faces on Australian paper money (*bibliography of banknotes*), the use of Jules Verne and Marcel Duchamp as respective literary and artistic links between France and Australia and France and the USA—with the difference that Duchamp lived in the United States, and his "readymades" are a commentary on the nature of the manufactured object on either side of the Atlantic ("Bicentenary Kit" pp. 175–76), whereas Verne never visited Australia, and is concerned not so much with objects as with "people".[29]

These are the kind of very general contrasts, echoes or parallels which the reader is likely to find because of the relatively high incidence of contiguity between "Letters from the Antipodes" and the sections concerned. But just as the irony of the Brisbane airport incident is set up by passages fifty pages apart, contiguity is by no means the only vehicle for relationships, although it is a powerful one. "Thematic echoes" may occur anywhere: "Transatlantic Carnival" begins with Nice's answer to the *Adelaide Advertiser*, in the form of a series of dalliance advertisements (pp. 54 and 56); while motivated thematic echoes are set up in two ways: by the use of "dreams"; and onomastically, through a whole network of names and authors or the place-names on the wall map in the narrator's room in college.

The onomastic procedure is an interesting one, but by no means new, since *Mobile* had already made extensive use of names as a means of setting up correspondences. Each section of *Boomerang* contains quotations from one or more French authors, whose names are given in capitals: Bataille in "The Ceremony I Missed", Barthes, Bougainville, Breton, Claudel, Diderot, Segalen, Verne in "Archipelago Shopping", and so on.[30] Some are writers who have travelled, others, travellers who have written. "Letters from the Antipodes" contains quotations from Bougainville, Breton and Verne, and one of the many ways of travelling round Butor's book from a base in "Letters from the Antipodes" is to use their capitalized names as signposts: Verne and Breton in "Archipelago Shopping" and Bougainville here and in "Transatlantic Carnival". A similar but more limited itinerary is provided by the wall map. As the narrator goes round the map—a kind of history and geography of the Pacific for schoolchildren—the names of some of the explorers mentioned in the extracts from Bougainville recur, while the whole region, and particularly the islands

166

of Melanesia, Micronesia and Polynesia, is rapidly presented. We are thus led "sideways" to other parts of "Letters from the Antipodes", and "outwards", to parts of the Pacific, and especially Tahiti, evoked in "Archipelago Shopping". But we are led outwards and sideways precisely because of the presence (here: visual, the wall map) of other places within our own, just as in "Transatlantic Carnival" the narrator buys three postcards in the Geneva anthropology museum, representing a Zuni katchina, a bark-painting from Arnhem Land and a mat used in Brazilian initiation ceremonies, before looking at two Tsimshian totem poles brought to Geneva from the Northwest coast of Canada (pp. 218,231).

In the "dreams", the narrator, sometimes called MB, experiences a variety of adventures related by rewritten extracts from the sections to which they refer, the rewriting consisting mainly of altering the grammatical person where necessary from third to first. Each of the sections, apart from the two "accompanying" ones, "Jungle" and "Nouvelles Indes Galantes", contains six dreams, and is referred to once in each of the four others. The four sections concerned are thus "receptive" and "radiating" in this respect, and perhaps for once the reader should throw linguistic caution to the winds and savour the humorous fantasies involving one Michel Butor as a lion ("Letters from the Antipodes", pp. 210-11: *red jungle dream*), or as a leprous youth who smells so strongly that his own parents abandon him . . . but who marries a princess in the end ("Transatlantic Carnival" p.349: *NW rainbow dream*, referring to a legend in "The Ceremony I Missed"), before musing on the status of material presented as part of a letter ("Letters from the Antipodes", p.20) and subsequently re-used as a dream ("Transatlantic Carnival" p.56: *Antipodean rainbow dream*).

7.2 Encounters and Echoes: Within "Letters from the Antipodes"

The previous section has tried to give some indication of how "Letters from the Antipodes" might relate to the book from which it has been so brutally excised. How it relates depends largely on how it—and the other sections—are read, since all kinds of partial readings are possible, based on colours, sections, or strands within sections.[31] How relationships within the section work also depends largely on what one chooses to read: there is no reason why one should not decide to concentrate on the various perspectives on Aboriginal society, for instance, before turning to the (re)presentation of white Australia. Nevertheless, the coexistence on each page of up to twelve separate strands, some of which may occur more than once, suggests that it might most profitably be treated as a unit. As a unit, it is situated within a block of up to seven pages, and may be preceded by or precede a page from another block, with which it may "dialogue". Page 433 begins "*come to the rescue of the unfortunate travellers*", while the last line of the previous page, which concludes "Bicentenary Kit", runs as follows: "blue because "blue Peter" is for *sailors the flag of distress*" (my italics). A double thematic bond is thus set up: "the flag of distress' and an appeal to other "sailors/travellers" to "come to the rescue". The relationship is not fortuitous, since the "blue Peter" is in fact the *departure* flag, and is described as such in the original version of *Bicentenary Kit*. The page may also dialogue with other parts of its own section, either directly, by means of the kind of contiguity just described, or less directly, by the continuation of one or more of its strands, or by echo or contrast with other pages. Within it, relationships may be of a visual nature (p.95: the dates), syntactic (p.285), or what is normally known as thematic.[32]

As an example of these relationships, the fifth block (pp.81–87) has been chosen for analysis.[32] It brings together thirteen strands, which combine to form various overlapping thematic kernels: the Aborigines (strands B,C,G,H,I,J,K,L); travel, including migration and exploration (A,E,G,K); and white Australia (F.H.M), thus giving considerable prominence to the Aborigines. Page 81 is framed by two presentations introduced by identical syntactic structures or 'isotaxies': "on the wall of my room in college... seascape at Sunset"/"on the back of a bark painting a pregnant woman"; the first develops the theme of migration, taken up again on pages 85 and 86, and is further related to the second by two "metaphorical isotopes" which highlight the limits of translation: the associations set up between the French "mer au coucher" (seascape at [sun-]set) and "femme enceinte" (pregnant woman) based on the pun implicit in "mer" (mère" = mother) and, by association with this pun and "enceinte"/"accouchement" (giving birth), plus a further possible one between "raie" (stinging-ray) and "Soleil": a partial rhyme which engenders "rayon" (ray) by a process of semantic association. If this is not apparent in English, then other associations are, for instance, repetitions: the "isographic" and "isophonic", "far/far" and "red/red"; the themes of disappearance and flight: "sunset"/"one day when he was hunting he tried to flee from a storm... before he could reach his crevice"/"In a few seconds he disappeared in the dense foliage"; sharpness: "lance"/
"axe"/"spines"; and above all, the animality of the Aborigines as seen by the Whites, and the human-like (and human) nature of the animal-spirits seen by the Aborigines: "the animal... the ape"/"the harmless little mimi Gradau is covered in hair... one day he threw his lance"/"far away... Dijalmung... has the body and head of a snake, and arms and legs like a human" (pp.81–82).

Page 82 picks up the themes of exploration (Bougainville) and disappearance ("then disappeared"/"had disappeared in a shipwreck"), giving the latter a new semantic layer by associating it with death: the context of the pieces just quoted, followed by the Cook: "last night seaman Torby Sutherland departed this life", and heralded by the Aboriginal legend: "as he dances round a grave ... decorated with a cross". Butor has departed from his source, Fearn-Wannan, substituting "âme" ("soul", or "heart and soul") for the word "leader" in the original text, so as to reinforce this particular association. Pages 83 and 84 offer a less dense network of semantic, syntactic and graphic correspondences between strands (correspondences within strands are not our concern here), largely because they are composed of only two, both concerning the Aborigines, one from Cook's diaries, the other from the Unesco exhibition booklet, with the sparse precision of the latter—in respect of hair, for instance—contrasting with the compassionate impressionism of the former. Page 85 takes up the themes of migration and exploration, with the exploratory passages framing the page, which is given a definite visual flavour by a number of geographic abbreviations (NNE,S,TAS, WA,WA,NW,SE,NW) and dates (8–21 October; 8–14 October; 20 June 1764, 28 November 1765, 24 February 1766, (ninth of May)).

One metaphorical isotope which works in English, although in an amusingly different way from the French, concerns the Fearn-Wannan and the bark painting; in the French, "subtiliser des bœufs et des moutons ... monté sur un cheval blanchâtre"/"Les lignes blanches ... sont le sillage" sets up a correspondence between the "lignes blanches" (white lines of foam) and "moutons" (sheep), reinforced by "blanchâtre" ("mouton" in French is, in a nautical context, "white horse"). The correspondence works in English because of "whitish horse" and "wake" ("sillage"). On page 86, the theme of death is carried on from page 82 ("otherwise we die slowly"/"when one of us dies"), along with migration (the wallmap); the isographic and isophonic "far away" is repeated, while "on the other side of the other end of the world without end" is one of a series of leitmotifs of varying complication mentioned in the introduction which runs through the entire section. Page 87 sets up, within the general framework of travel, an amusing contrast between the prospective: "I leave again ... for Sydney so that I can meet you at the airport on the morning of the 4th" and the present tense of the *red Archipelago dream*": "I go with a friend and his wife to meet you at Sydney airport ... You're not there", which in turn refers outward to the "real" passage in "Archipelago Shopping" (p.65). And just as "Sydney" is a small isographic and isophonic reinforcement of the semantic process juxtaposing the two scenes at the airport, similarly "Adelaide" acts as a determining agent in the process generating[33] "Adelaide Advertiser", aided by a whole series of nouns with an initial capital: Airlines, Alitalia, Australians, ANTIPODES, ending with Angelique.

8. Themes

As each page refers at once "inwards" (the relationships between coexistent strands), "sideways" (these between it and other pages of the same block) and "outwards" (those between it and other blocks or sections), functioning as a unit within various contexts, any general themes one might like to discern within "Letters from the Antipodes" are clearly enriched and modified by comparison with other sections of *Boomerang*. However we react to the picture of the Australian Aborigine, our reaction will be at least somewhat different if we compare it with the presentation of the Northwest Coast Indian in "The Ceremony I Missed", the Polynesians in "Archipelago Shopping", the native Paraguayans in "Transatlantic Carnival" and, to a lesser extent, the American Indian in "Bicentenary Kit". In turn, these may all be compared with the idealized presentation of native peoples in the "Nouvelles Indes Galantes", where the eighteenth century noble savage vies in generosity with his European conquerors. To catalogue all the themes of the section would also be impossible, given the variety of ways in which it may be read (and the multiplicity of criteria for classification); it would also be undesirable, since the whole point of the book's "mobile" construction is to allow the reader to discover for himself. The present section is not meant to do the reader's work for him (whereas the justification for the preceding ones is that they should make it possible for him to work in a more meaningful context); rather, it raises some very general questions in respect of what are likely to be three major themes, whatever classificatory system is adopted, and in particular, the theme of travel.

If we take the theme of the Aborigine as our starting point, certain considerations seem unaffected by the problem of context. The first is simply the very high proportion of material in "Letters from the Antipodes" dealing with Aboriginal society. Ten of the thirty-two or thirty-five strands are wholly concerned with the history or present condition of the Aboriginal people, while several others touch upon these themes. *Boomerang* is the latest of a series of works by Butor, including *Mobile* and the second book in the "spirit of the place" series, *Où*, which celebrate the richness and dignity of so-called "primitive" civilizations that have been partially assimilated by more "advanced" ones. In the present work, the bark-painting and the legend it recounts are a testimony to the rich cultural heritage of the Australian Aborigine, with Butor's rewriting of the Mountford somewhat akin to the work of restoration in art—except that it is a "free" restoration, its aim being to add a new dimension, not just to bring back what is partially effaced.

This process of "pious profanation",[34] to use Butor's admirable terminology, is one attempt to redress the balance in the face of the neglect of a social kind described in "health problems", or the political neglect against which black voices are now protesting ("the red and black day"). For until very recently, black Australia did not speak or write itself: it had to be written or spoken about, by whites. One very striking contrast between black and white Australia in "Letters from the Antipodes" is that with the exception of "the red and black day", the direct Aboriginal voice is unheard (the legends are doubly transcribed), whereas white Australia speaks itself.

The manner of speaking is extremely diverse, from the vulgarized presentation of Cook's journals to the massage parlour advertisements and the narratorial voice(s). If the narratorial voice is sympathetic, and fascinated by Australian nature ("Marie-Jo darling") and by what it regards as a dynamic society ("talk"), certain extracts seem rather at odds with this, presenting a hedonistic ("islands in the Sun"), sex-obsessed ("small ads") people, with a strong element of the bizarre ("memorial to Raymond Roussel"; "the principality"): another variety of the Great Australian Stupor. White Australia may even appear less *serious* than black Australia. This is partly true, and it may be no bad thing either. Australian society is often regarded as excessively conformist and dull, with no place for even the harmless eccentric. The little old lady of the "camera obscura" and the self-styled Prince Leonard have in common an endearing alliance of commercial good sense and eccentricity which render a visit to Toowoomba or Hutt River Province as potentially rewarding (for them and for us) as a stay on one of the "islands in the Sun". On the other hand, the massage parlour phenomenon is neither trivial nor eccentric (although clearly very good business), but a frightening testimony to the unliberated state of our sexual *mores*, which have been devastatingly analyzed in a recent book by Ronald Conway, one of our more persuasive prophets of doom.[35]

The third major theme is travel, in many of its manifestations: exploration (Cook, the narrator, "Australia unlimited"), wandering (the narrator on occasions), moving (Toby Ginger), or tourism ("islands in the Sun", the narrator). With it of course goes the act of inscription, whether it be writing, in the case of the narrator or Cook, or painting, in the case of the Aboriginal children's paintings on the theme of their travels. From her home, Hermannsburg, little Sandra has represented Alice Springs as a great blue whirling mass (p.447). For the author of "gaps", it is, in retrospect, the five bars[36] of the Stuart Arms pub (p.443).

171

This difference may help us further to refine the notion of the place, which may be seen not only as a radiating or receiving point, but also—possibly as a variation of the receiving-point—as a *vantage-point* from which to observe other places. Michel Butor has described the role of Australia in this respect as follows: "Australia is for me a "sensitive" place where general changes in the world are expressed in a particularly interesting way. It's a place where you can listen to the rest of the world, above all through the intermediary of its artists and writers"[37]—our very remoteness (or the remoteness of other places from us: Butor's villa at Nice is named "The Antipodes") puts us in a highly privileged position in respect to the rest of the world. Michel Butor's travels are partly a result of, partly a search for, dis-orientation (the East, and particularly Egypt has haunted him since *Passage de Milan*, written in 1954), a series of perspectives on past and contemporary Western society. Researched in Australia, and largely written in France, "Letters from the Antipodes" presents us with the ready-made perspective of a French narrator, and the material for other perspectives in the form of a highly unusual "kit"—the other thematic strands—since there is more than one way of assembling it.[38] To these we bring our own perspective, which modifies and is modified by the text, either "becoming slightly Australian" (p.439) if we are not, or, from our Australian vantage point, viewing the rest of the world with slightly different eyes. And for those of us who can read French—unhappily, an apparently diminishing group in Australia—a further tonic of disorientation awaits as we begin our journey around the world of *Boomerang*.

9. Gaps

"Four o'clock BARTHES perhaps". This cryptic reference to the author of *The Empire of Signs* ("Archipelago Shopping", p.204) invites us to search for extracts from his book on Japan. There are none. Nor, according to the narrator, has he himself really yet succeeded in writing about it (Archipelago Shopping", p.289). Nor again has he succeeded in writing about golf in Australia, or toilets and their graffiti, the lost treasures, or the depths of the red desert (pp. 276-77): the many "gaps" in "Letters from the Antipodes".

To treat these as examples of failure would be to oversimplify. The quotations from "Letters from the Antipodes" are retrospective in nature, while these from "Archipelago Shopping" are prospective, suggesting that one day the book on Japan will be written. This is highly likely, and it will probably be called "the spirit of the place, IV", bringing together Japan and Mexico, linked by the theme of exploration. But beyond this informational point, there lies a more complex issue which has already been touched on briefly. It concerns the idea of "incompleteness", and relates to the unusual construction of *Boomerang*, the work-as-score to be "played" by the reader

The notion of the "incomplete" or "unfinished" book is by no means a new one in Butor, and can be found as early as *Passing Time*, written some years (1956) before the first of the "mobile" works. For Butor, "finished" and "closed" are synonymous: the "closed" book presents itself, or is presented, as complete and authoritative, a "last word" preventing any new ones from being written, a brick in the edifice of moribund literature constituting a kind of library-prison.[39] "Traditional" works such as novels by Balzac are potentially closed, partly because they have engendered a whole school or style of writing persisting to the present day and amply fulfilling the reader's expectations about what a novel ought to contain ("real life" characters, interesting descriptions and plot, to mention three of the most common features). In short, they present no challenge, and are a conservative, self-perpetuating force. They not only inhibit new readings of books written in their mould, but of themselves, since they are the authority behind (before) the school, which acts as a kind of guarantee for this authority in a nicely circular process. They can, however, be "opened" by new critical approaches, and for this in France one has to thank the salutary example of the "new novel", which—because it *cannot* be read like a novel by Balzac—has led to new readings of old novels.[40]

On the other hand, there is the work whose "incompleteness" indicates its potentiality, structured so as to provide the reader with a degree of freedom within a rigid framework, a work organizing chance—and thus verging on the *game*.[41] In this respect it is interesting to note that the recorded version of Butor and Henri Pousseur's "opera", *Votre Faust*, comes with all the paraphernalia of a game—board, dice and so on—and can be "played" in two senses of the word. In modern musical terminology, *Votre Faust*, and works such as *Boomerang*, are "overdetermined". As Pousseur has put it in an essay on music, they are "not *indetermined*, but rather *indeterminable*, for the simple reason that [they are] too rich and too pregnant to be characterized by a single definition . . . [they are] thus literally *overdetermined*" (his italics).[42] The overdetermination of *Boomerang* stems from the structuring concept: a large number of heterogeneous elements (the sections, strands within sections, colours) are brought together and combined on the page according to a whole series of "rules"—the sequence of colours, sections, strands within sections—and thus allow the kinds of textual journeys and encounters that have been outlined. It is confusing only if the rules are not understood, and its major difference from so-called "traditional"

173

works is that reading the latter has come to be seen as a natural activity because of the conventions within which they work and the expectations the reader brings to them.[43] It is an ambitious work, and no doubt on first reading a highly disconcerting one. More than with most works perhaps, whether it is a rewarding one depends on the reader.

Michael Spencer

Notes

1. Michel Butor, "Le Voyage et l'écriture", in *Répertoire IV* (Paris: Editions de Minuit, 1974), pp. 9–29. All the quotations in this paragraph are taken from the same essay.
2. *Répertoire II* (Paris: Editions de Minuit, 1964), p.49, essay on "L'Espace du roman".
3. See the essay "Le Livre comme objet", in *Répertoire II*, pp.104–23 and my remarks in section 2.
4. *Répertoire III* (Paris: Editions de Minuit, 1968), p.9, essay on "La Critique et l'invention".
5. *In OEuvres complètes* (Paris: Pléiade, 1945), pp.378–82.
6. "Le Livre comme objet", p. 107.
7. *Répertoire III*, p. 401, essay on "La Littérature, l'oreille et l'œil".
8. For the concept of "open-ness", see my *Michel Butor* (New York: Twayne, 1974), pp. 26–29, and section 9. On "serial" works, see Antoine Compagnon, *La Seconde Main ou le travail de la citation* (Paris: Editions du Seuil, 1979), pp. 382 *passim*.
9. "In the symphony formed by the whole there's a kind of double percussion, with the Jungle as a deep percussion, like the timpani in an orchestra, and then a kind of light percussion like cymbals or a triangle, and this is "Les Nouvelles Indes Galantes" (Michel Butor in an interview with the translator, *Malahat Review*, 56 (October 1980): 77–92.
10. George Bataille, "La Part maudite" in *OEuvres Complètes* (Paris: Gallimard, 1976).
11. Michel Butor and Jacques Monory, *Bicentenaire Kit* (Paris: Club Français du Meilleur Livre, 1976). The only copy of this limited-edition "box" known to be in Australia is in the University of Queensland Fine Arts Museum.
12. Michel Butor, *Réseau aérien* (Paris: Gallimard, 1962).
13. Alan Moorehead, *The Fatal Impact* (Harmondsworth: Penguin, 1968). For Tahitian society in 1820, see pp. 110–13.
14. For some examples, see section 7.1.
15. pp. 90, 96, 145, 146, 159–60, 307, 371–72, 401–2.
16. The frequency is as follows: A–34; B–64; C–28; D–6; E–31; F–47; G–30; H–25 or 23; I–27; J–14; K–24; L–24; M–22; N–23; O–16; P–17; Q–18;

R–16; S–14; T–13; U–11; V–11; W–8; X–8 or 7; Y–9; Z–6 or 5; UU–4; VV–5; WW–3; XX–2; YY–3; ZZ–1. The differing figures in respect of H, Z and X are due to the fact that on p.369 and 433 H forms a "composite" strand with Z and X respectively.

17. To give one example of deliberate alteration, the Aboriginal organization "One People of Australia League" has been changed to "One People of Australia Limited" (p.186), the world "limited" setting up a quite different semantic resonance from "league".

18. Compagnon, *La Seconde Main*, p.29. This is by far the fullest study of quotation ever to appear. For quotation in Butor, see Françoise Van Rossum-Guyon, "Aventures de la citation chez Butor", in *Butor, Colloque de Cerisy* (Paris: U.G.E., Coll. 10/18, 1974), pp. 17–39.

19. For a hilarious discussion of the apparatus of footnotes see Compagnon, pp.339–41 (including footnotes).

20. Laurent Jenny, "La Stratégie de la forme", *Poétique*, 27 (1976): 257–81.

21. Thus writes *our* authority, Compagnon, pp. 361–62.

22. Jorge Luis Borges, *Fictions* (Paris: Gallimard, Coll. "Folio"), pp. 71–72.

23. See Compagnon, pp. 392–93.

24. Contemporary French criticism distinguishes (at least) between the author-as-man ("l'auteur"), the author-as-writer ("le scripteur") and the narrator (the recounting voice). See J.-P. Goldenstein, *Lire le roman* (Brussels: A. de Boek/Duculot, 1980), pp. 28–32. A further distinction has also been proposed between "recounting" and "seeing". See G. Genette, *Figures III* (Paris: Seuil, 1972), sections on "mode" and "voix".

25. See Françoise Van Rossum-Guyon, p.21. The notion of uniqueness is, however, tenacious. An erudite paper by S. Morawski on the history and practice of quotation nevertheless manages to suggest that it is somehow morally wrong to quote: "The artist proffers his OWN vision since he wants to create the world anew. Accordingly he dissociates himself from quotations since every INDIVIDUAL WHOLE is to be a once-only product": paper entitled "The Basic Functions of Quotation", in *Sign, Language, Culture*, ed. Greimas *et al.* The Hague: Mouton, 1970), pp. 690–705. Quotation p.704.

26. Interview in *L'Arc*, 39 (1969): 2.

27. Jean-Paul Sartre, *Qu'est ce que la littérature?* (Paris: Gallimard, Coll. "Idées"), p.59 *et seq.*

28. The text is in fact "unfinished" or "open". See section 9.

29. Contrast the extracts on Aboriginal art by the other French writer quoted in "Letters from the Antipodes", André Breton, with those of Jules Verne on Aborigines.

30. Non-French authors are also found, such as Butler and Melville, and a similar but more limited network is thereby created.

31. This may partially justify our own amputation.

32. "Isotopic" would be a more precise and more useful term. What follows owes a great deal to (a) François Rastier, "Systématique des Isotopies", in A.-J. Greimas, ed., *Essais de sémiotique poétique* (Paris: Larousse, Coll. "L", 1972), pp. 80–106; and (b) J.-M. Adam and J.-P Goldenstein, *Linguistique et discours littéraire* (Paris: Larousse, Coll. "L", 1976), pp. 97–107.

33. Generative devices, or phonemes, words, sentences, even whole episodes "producing" or determining other phonemes, words etc. are extremely common in modern French literature. For the generative process, see Alain Robbe-Grillet, "Sur le choix des générateurs", *Nouveau roman: hier, aujourd'hui* (U.G.E., Coll. 10/18, 1972), II: 157–62, or, within the same volume, Jean Ricardou, "Naissance d'une fiction": 379–92.

34. *Répertoire II*, p.240 (essay on "Victor Hugo romancier").

35. *Land of the Long Weekend* (Melbourne: Sun Books, 1978), chapter IV: "Sex à la Mode".

36. The original has five "pubs", which is obviously an error.

37. Interview with Michael Spencer, *Meanjin* 2 (1980): 231.

38. See interview with Michael Spencer in the *Malahat Review*: "I've often explained that my books could be considered as models . . . the word "kit" in "Bicentenary Kit" is used . . . with the meaning it has in the toy trade or in hobbying: a unit which enables you to make a scale model of something, a portable model of a reality which is much more difficult to grasp when it has its normal dimensions" (p.81).

39. "Victor Hugo romancier", in *Répertoire II*, p.240.

40. The difference between "open" and "closed" is akin to Barthes's distinction between the "readable" and the "writable" book. See Roland Barthes, *S/Z* (Seuil, Coll. "Points", 1970), pp. 10–12.

41. For a fuller treatment of these notions, see my *Michel Butor*, pp. 28–31 and especially the section on *Votre Faust*, pp. 132–40.

42. Henri Pousseur, "The Question of Order in New Music", *Perspectives of New Music* (Fall–Winter 1960), pp. 107–8.

43. Jonathan Culler, *Structuralist Poetics* (London: Routledge, 1966), chapter seven: "Convention and Naturalization."

Index

Order of appearance of textual strands, by page. To be read in conjunction with graph p.156 and key to strands pp. 158–60.

369, B^2–H/Z–T–G–U–F
370, F–V–E–W–C–X–B–Y–A
371, A–UU–A
372, A–Z–B–Y
373, Y–C–X–E–W–F
374, F–V–G–U–H–T
375, I–B^2

378, B^2–J–S–K–R
379, R–B–^{1}Q–L–P–M–F^1–N
*380, N–?–VV–O–F^1–N–P
381, M–Q–L–R–B^1
382, B^1–S–K–B^2–J–T–I
383, I–U–V–G–W–F–X–E
384, E–Y–C–Z

401, Z–B–UU–A
402, A–WW–A
403, A–VV–B
404, B–UU–C–Z–E–Y
405, Y–F–X–G–W–H–V

412, V–I–U–J–T–K–B2
413, B^2–B^1–S–L
414, L–R–M–Q–N–P–Q–F^1–D–XX
*415, XX–F^1–P–?–Q–N–R–M–S–L

416, L–B^2–B^1–T–K–U

433, U–J–V–I–W–H/X–G–Y–F
434, F–Z–E–UU–C–VV
435, VV–B–WW
436, WW–A–YY
437, YY–A–XX–B
438, B–WW–C
439, C–VV–E

442, E–N–F–Z–G–Y–X–I–W
443, W–J–V–K–U–B^1–T
444, T–L–B^2–M–S–N–R
*445, R–?–Q–F^1–P–ZZ–P–Q–F^1–?–S–N–B^2
446, B^2–M–T–L–R–B^1–V–K–W
447, W–J–X–I–Y–H–Z–G–F–VV
448, E–G–C–B–A

*very short strands, source not identified, as follows:
p. 380 "how are you getting on Toby Ginger".
p.415 "how is your dream going. John McNeil".
p.445 "how far have you got John McNeil at the other end, what has happened to your dream".
p.445 "how far have you got, Toby Ginger, other world, what's become of your dream".

DATE DUE

DEMCO 38-297